Praise for *Great Connections* by Anne Baber and Lynne Waymon:

"HIGHLY RECOMMENDED."
—*The Midwest Book Review*

"GIVES BUSINESSPEOPLE THE TOOLS to naturally generate leads and referrals through networking. Tremendously practical."
—CURT KOWALSKI, President, The Team Network, Inc., Washington, D.C.

"THE AUTHORS' REFRESHING APPROACH gives you a competitive edge in today's tough job market."
—JANICE Y. BENJAMIN, Kansas City, Coauthor of the *How to Be Happily Employed* series

"PRACTICAL, STRAIGHTFORWARD, AND WITHOUT A HARD-SELL."
—*Career Opportunity News*

HOW TO FIREPROOF YOUR CAREER

SURVIVAL STRATEGIES FOR VOLATILE TIMES

Anne Baber and Lynne Waymon

BERKLEY BOOKS, NEW YORK

HOW TO FIREPROOF YOUR CAREER

A Berkley Book / published by arrangement with
the authors

PRINTING HISTORY
Berkley edition / May 1995

For information address: The Berkley Publishing Group,
200 Madison Avenue, New York, New York 10016.

ISBN: 0-425-14731-2

BERKLEY®
Berkley Books are published by The Berkley Publishing Group,
200 Madison Avenue, New York, New York 10016.
BERKLEY and the "B" design
are trademarks belonging to Berkley Publishing Corporation.

PRINTED IN THE UNITED STATES OF AMERICA

10 9 8 7 6 5 4 3 2 1

Contents

HOW TO FIREPROOF YOUR CAREER

SURVIVAL STRATEGIES FOR VOLATILE TIMES

Part I

Volatile Times

Chapter 1

Running Scared

The number one fear of middle-class Americans is unemployment. In one poll, it even outranked drugs and crime. For the first time in our lives, joblessness is hitting close to home. Long after government officials declared the eighty-something recession over, one family in ten still has someone out of work. One-half of all workers know someone who has lost a job. One-third expect someone in their families to be laid off in the next twelve months. No wonder we're anxious.

Our sense of security didn't evaporate overnight. Our fear didn't begin with cataclysmic events, like the Great Depression's stock market crash and executives leaping out of windows. Our fear has grown slowly since the mid-eighties, fed by thousands of newspaper headlines about layoffs at America's premiere companies and jobs gone south or overseas. Our fear leaps into our throats when we see a for sale sign on the house down the block or get a phone call from an old friend who wonders if we know of any job opportunities.

We used to feel safe, but the things that protected us in the past—a college education, seniority, being a good employee—don't seem to protect people anymore. We're not sure if anything can.

Most of all, we desperately want to make sure that—no matter what happens to our jobs—we can continue to make a living.

That's what this book is all about.

It's not about job security, although many of the ideas you'll learn might help you hang onto your job, even in tough times. It's about career security. In the years to come, career security—your ability to earn a living—must replace job security—your dependence on your employer.

This book is not for people who are unemployed, although much of the information will be useful to those who have lost their jobs. It's for people who are still employed but who are worried as never before about what the future holds.

You may not be able to avoid being laid off. Many competent, capable, loyal, enthusiastic, hardworking, well-educated employees have been and will be let go. Career consultants predict that we will change careers three or four times and have as many as thirteen different jobs during our work lives. Only half of those job changes will be voluntary. In other words, people who are entering the workforce now can expect to go through the experience of job loss as many as six or seven times. If you are at the halfway mark in your career, you could still be displaced three or four times before you retire.

Amazingly, more than 80 percent of people who lose their jobs nowadays are surprised—and unprepared. We wrote this book to prevent that.

You have a choice. You can sit back, wait, and worry. If your job disappears, you can react after the fact, when everything you need to do to cope and regain your ability to earn a living is much harder. Or, you can be prepared. You can be proactive and set in motion today the plans that will protect you tomorrow.

We call this new approach fireproofing your career.

Tom* wishes he had protected himself . . . before he was laid off. He has some advice for you.

*Although we quote real people, only their first names have been used.

The Case of the Not-So-Bulletproof Manager

"I thought I was bulletproof," Tom says. "As manager of administrative services for a large oil company, I had a staff of 100 and a budget of $15 million. I had great ratings and a high salary. And, looking back, I can see I'd gotten too comfortable.

"I thought, 'How can I get fired? They need my services. I'm the only one who can do my job. This is the only company I've ever worked for and they appreciate my loyalty. I'm safe.'

"Actually, I felt so secure that I didn't even notice that I was thinking this way. I just thought like that.

"Then, out of the blue, my position was eliminated. The emotional trauma was unbelievable. In the first few days after I got the news, I even explored the idea of suicide. I would review the events, and I'd think, 'Yeah, my wife and kids could collect the insurance and be safe.' Now, I see that I was still looking for safety outside myself. At the ripe old age of fifty, after twenty-seven years with one company, I was completely out of touch with my identity as a person with skills, with value. If the company didn't need me, I reasoned, then nobody did.

"Now, six months later, one of the most amazing things to me is that none of my friends or past coworkers has tried to learn from my experience. During this entire six months, no one has asked, 'So what's your advice to all of us who haven't been laid off yet, but might be? What have you learned? What do you wish you'd done differently?'

"This has been such a wake-up experience, and I've had to learn so much, that I'm full of advice. But isn't it strange no one asks? My boss was laid off two weeks ago. With just the two of us laid off, the company has saved more than $215,000 in salaries. I could even give him some advice.

"I have three suggestions.

"First, realize a layoff can, and probably will, happen to you. Two years ago, I would have told you, 'I'll be the last to leave. The day the CEO leaves, I'll be the guy who turns out the light after the door closes behind him.' Now, I know nobody's invincible.

"Second, learn your way around a computer. As a manager, I had people working for me who were experts in Lotus and WordPerfect. So, I thought I'd never need those skills. But, in the small to midsize companies that are hiring now, interviewers ask me, 'Are you technically competent? We don't have the support staff you were used to.' So I've been playing catch-up.

"Third, build a network by doing favors for others. When I was laid off, I didn't have a network. I had a few friends inside and outside the corporation, but we didn't *do* anything for each other, really. It's taken me six months of reaching out and giving to others to begin to get a snowball effect where people are looking out for opportunities for me in return. The more you give to others, the more you get. Seems like I should have known that, but I didn't."

Create a New Definition of Security

To begin fireproofing ourselves, we need a new, expanded definition of security. We've grown up with a definition that led us to believe that security was a job that ended with a gold watch and a pension. Your job today is much more likely to end with a pink slip and a severance check.

Today, security does not mean predictability or lack of change. Today, the most secure workers have new skills and attitudes that allow them to take charge of change and invent their own future.

Your security is in your own head. Security is your mindset, your capabilities, your expertise.

Your security is the result of good planning, flexibility, and multiple options.

Your security is having the resources—personal, intellectual, financial, and educational—to move on or up with or without your current employer.

No employer can give you this kind of security. You must create it for yourself. To create it, you must grapple with some tough truths and you must act in your own best interest.

Face Facts, Protect Yourself

The first section of this book, "Volatile Times," will help you face facts and become more aware of the concepts behind career security and how these concepts affect you. Some of the anxiety people are experiencing today comes from their lack of understanding about what's happening in the economy. Some of the anxiety is produced by outworn assumptions about work. Some comes because people really haven't thought about what work means in their lives. As you read this book, you'll begin to understand the economic forces that are changing work in America. You'll be able to throw out old assumptions and supplant them with new ideas that will strengthen you. You will gain insight into your beliefs and attitudes and perhaps change your mind about some things.

As you take a hard look at the realities of today's workplace and job market, you'll find out:

- How secure your current job really is
- How much of your feelings of self-worth come from your job and how to reduce your dependency on that job
- How the language of layoffs takes its toll on your self-esteem
- How job loss affects people

These chapters pull no punches. We believe that, if you know what's going on, you'll be more likely to be motivated to make the changes that will eventually provide you with the kind of protection you need. Even if you begin to feel anxious, keep reading. You will be able to put that anxiety to good use as you take action to fireproof your career.

If the economists and workforce experts are right, tough times won't be over soon. The American economy is undergoing a permanent change. As many as half of all the jobs that have disappeared in the last ten years will never return. As you manage your career during this time of unprecedented change, your awareness of yourself, your type of job, your company, your industry, and the process of job loss will provide some protection for you. Forewarned is forearmed. The worst thing you can do is pretend that things will get better and hope that, if you ignore what's going on, it will go away.

More than three years after she was laid off, Joanne is still coping with the psychological fallout of job loss. Though she's done almost everything right, she still is groping for a way to be committed to a job without being co-opted by it.

The Case of the Uncommitted Heart

"I canceled everything for the weekend: dinner with my sister, a movie with a friend," says Joanne. "I decided to sit on my deck and think until I'd figured out why I don't want to take a another job, don't even want to interview for a job.

"I was laid off more than three years ago, and I can't bring myself to get a job. I have skillfully avoided the problem of finding a job. I went back to school to get an MBA, and I supplemented my paychecks for part-time work with money from my savings. So, for a long time, I could rationalize not looking for work.

"I even interviewed for and was offered some jobs that other people would consider very good jobs, but I found something wrong with them.

"So, there I was on the deck, thinking, asking myself, 'What's wrong?'

"It's hard to be laid off. Actually, my job as director of real estate planning was eliminated, but the result is the same. There's a lot of social denial. It's like you have a contagious disease. People don't want to talk about it, share about it. It's like a death; people don't know how to handle it, so they don't say anything. It's worse than that: They have to believe you did something wrong and deserved getting fired. If they can believe that, then they don't have to believe it could happen to them.

"You feel invisible. When the government came out with unemployment figures, I thought, 'and they're not even counting me. They're not counting all the people who are disenchanted with work, like me, who have dropped out.'

"But that weekend, I finally figured out why I was stuck, why I couldn't bear the idea of looking for a job, why I'd even turned down jobs.

"I had given my heart and soul to the company that laid me off. I contributed years of hard work and something of value, and the company betrayed me. That's the right word—betrayal. I'm amazed at how deep that hurt is, even three years later. I wonder, 'If I take another job, can I trust the company I'm working for?'

"It's very frightening. I know they can trust me. I'll be loyal, hardworking, intelligent, ethical. But can I trust them? I'm not going to be betrayed again, but I'm worried I won't see it coming, because I'll be working so hard to be a model employee. Can I back off? Is there a place to be the kind of employee I want to be without being so wrapped up that I don't see what's going on?

"What if I don't give my all? What if I work only forty hours a week? Won't I be only average? I don't want to be average, but I do want to keep a balance. I've learned that in the last three years. Yet, can I keep that balance and still be considered outstanding? What I see is, you must sacrifice to be a success, but if you sacrifice, you may be nothing more than a chump. You may be setting yourself up. There just aren't any role models of successful people who don't make the sacrifices.

"I don't want my next job to be just a job. Work is such a big part of our lives. But I don't want to allow myself to be consumed. I just don't know how to work for an organization without being consumed by it. And that's too dangerous.

"I have figured out that much. I still haven't determined what kind of relationship I can have with a company that won't leave me vulnerable."

Awareness of yourself, the messages about work in our culture, and the phenomena of job loss is not enough. There also are specific plans you should be making now and steps you should begin to take today.

As you read this book, take notes, jot down your answers to the questions in the chapters, make lists of things to do, and collect information. You may want to buy a notebook and keep it with you as you read.

The second section of this book, "Survival Strategies," will help you get moving to take charge of your own career and protect yourself. In this part of the book, you'll learn five strategies that will help you fireproof your career. You'll discover:

- Why you need to become psychologically self-employed and how to do it
- What you should be doing to take care of yourself and your family financially
- How to increase your mastery of your job or begin to develop expertise in new or related career fields
- How to broaden your career options, even if you've always worked in a narrow, specialized field
- Why you should network now, while you're still employed, and how to do it effectively, both inside and outside your workplace

As you implement these strategies in your own life, they may help you keep your job. They certainly will help you cope if your job disappears. They also will put you on the fast track to get a new—perhaps even a better—job.

Chapter 11 will help you craft your own career security plan. The action steps include both things to think about and things to do. These activities are designed to help you change the way you think about work. They outline the steps you must take to protect yourself. So, don't just read this book, put the strategies into action in your life.

What would you do if you lost your job tomorrow? We hope you will have longer than that to prepare yourself, because some of the strategies, such as creating a viable network, will take you several months, and others are multi-year efforts, such as getting a graduate degree or saving enough to tide you over. Many fireproofing steps, however, can be accomplished quickly. Once you create your personal career security plan, you can refer to it again and again and update it, if necessary, as you continue to manage your career.

Chapter 12 contains a list of resources, so you can go on learning from a variety of experts.

Cornelia wishes she'd taken action before she was laid off. She realizes now that she had abdicated planning her career and, worse yet, allowed her company's attitudes to restrict her vision of her future.

The Case of the Complacent Couch Potato

"I was lazy," says Cornelia. "Oh, I wouldn't have admitted to being lazy, if you'd accused me of it. But, I remember, now, that when my friend Tony told me he'd enrolled for his master's degree, I said to myself, 'Not me. I'm tired when I get home. I'm happy just relaxing and watching TV or reading. I'm not going to go to all that work when it won't make a bit of difference. They won't give me a raise if I have another degree. I won't get promoted if I have another degree.'

"I wasn't seeing the big picture. I was looking only at how more education might—or in the case of my company—might not win me a gold star. That attitude was really stupid, because what happened was, they laid me off. They laid the whole department off and consolidated customer information systems in Dallas.

"So, now I'm job hunting. Several times, I've been a finalist, but they chose somebody else, somebody with a master's. Now I've enrolled in school. If I'd done it while I was still working, the company would have paid for most of it. Guess who's paying for it now? Me. Right. I don't have time to be lazy now. I'm working two part-time jobs to keep bread on the table, and I'm going to school. I sure made sure I did it the hard way!

"Advice? I could give advice till the cows come

home. Here's what I say: You don't necessarily get more education for your current job; you get more education so you can compete with people for your next job. One more thing: The less demanding your current job is, the more you need to keep your skills up to date. I was a couch potato both off and on the job. It was stupid to let a company that didn't value education make me think education wasn't valuable."

Listen to the Experts

Many of the experts quoted in this book are ordinary people, like Tom and Joanne and Cornelia, who have suffered the trauma of termination. As career coaches, we've worked with many clients who were reeling from the blow of being laid off. Throughout the book are stories and suggestions from these people about what they did wrong and what they did right.

We've also quoted people who have coped effectively with being unemployed, who have "survived" organizational convulsions, or who have moved into new jobs, even new careers. Many of these copers had intuitively begun to protect their careers and livelihoods and were eager to share their ideas and experiences. Their stories and creative solutions will inspire you and challenge you.

As consultants, workshop leaders, and speakers, we've seen inside some of America's biggest corporations and government organizations. We know what's happening as employers and employees try to deal with new economic realities that make new workplace relationships imperative. Organizations are floundering and employees are frustrated and fearful.

We have some other relevant experience: Both of us have been laid off. We "survived," changed careers, and our annual earnings quickly exceeded our previous secure salaries.

We came to the idea of fireproofing careers indirectly. Our first book, *Great Connections: Small Talk and Networking for Businesspeople,* led to our speaking to thousands of people in all kinds of organizations about how to build business relationships. We noticed something about these audiences. As the eighties ended, people were still concerned with climbing the ladder and getting ahead. Now, however, our audiences have changed. Now we're talking to more and more people who are unemployed or worried about being unemployed. Most of these people are not prepared at all for being let go, not prepared to cope with all that unemployment means, not prepared for job hunting. As we recognized their needs, we began to speak about fireproofing and teaching the skills in this book in workshops nationwide.

Most gratifying are the people who have heard us speak or participated in one of our workshops, taken the ideas to heart, begun to work on the strategies, and then written or called us to share their profound sense of relief and their conviction that, once again, they are in control of their careers and their lives. They've come up with some terrific ideas. We've quoted them, too.

Find Out What They're Not Telling You

Career security is still in the closet.

In a 1990 Conference Board survey, 70 percent of 216 major U.S. manufacturing and service firms said employees cannot rely on the company but must be self-sufficient about managing their careers within the firm or moving to another company if that furthers their objectives. Have you heard that from your company? There's quite a gap between what companies are thinking and what employees understand. In some companies, the message isn't getting out because management believes that without the carrot of job security dangling in front of them, employees will be less loyal, more likely to hop to another company. In some organizations, the message about self-sufficiency is such a departure from the paternalism of the past that they can't bring themselves to say it out loud because it contradicts what they have been telling employees for years. In many companies, the topic is too hot to handle. If corporate paternalism is dead, what is the new paradigm? How should employers and employees relate? What are reasonable expectations for employees to have about their careers? Most companies don't have any answers.

Your employer may not tell you to become psychologically self-employed. Oh, the company might send you to a course on empowerment, but would be surprised to see you applying it to your career. Frankly, dependent employees are obedient employees.

Your employer may not tell you to become an expert. Experts are people who change things. That's threatening even to companies that say they embrace change.

Your employer may not tell you to broaden your career, to move out of specialization. With the *up* disappearing out of *upward mobility,* companies don't know what to do with aspiring workers. As organizations flatten the hierarchy, the old career ladders are missing rungs. Today's careers are wayward, not upward, but who is choosing the way? Employees who have relied on their companies to point the direction and set them on a secure career path now feel lost and wonder where they will be able to go and how they will get there. Mobility within organizations is hampered by the high walls that surround various functional areas. There are unwritten rules about poaching and stealing another department's people. Turfs and the corporate culture that supports them sometimes make even talking with people in other departments difficult.

Your employer may not tell you to protect yourself financially, to start your own part-time business, or to moonlight. The golden handcuffs are very real. Companies know that dependency on that paycheck and the valuable benefits that accompany it keeps employees in line. Severance policies are shrouded in secrecy. It's difficult to get information about what to expect if your job goes away. The lack of knowledge makes job loss that much more terrifying. In many organizations, employees are expected to work longer and longer hours. How much of your life does a paycheck buy? As companies reduce headcount or hold off on hiring, some people are working eighty-two-hour weeks and doing the jobs of two or more people. When one man complained, his boss said, ''Do you want this job or not?'' It's a great deal for employers. They get two employees for the price of one.

Your employer may not tell you to network. Networking on the job is often considered *not* working, even though it can unclog bureaucratic bottlenecks and make getting the job done easier. Unless you are in sales, networking with people outside your company may not be valued very much, either. For employees in some companies, belonging to a professional organization at the international or national level is acceptable, but attending meetings of the local chapter is not. These companies fear that employees will spend too much time out of the office, compare their salaries and working conditions with those in other local companies, or uncover other opportunities through networking and jump ship.

There are companies that will tell you all of these things, but, in most organizations, career security is an emerging issue that hasn't yet been addressed.

People who have been laid off won't tell you about these strategies, either. It's not that they don't want to, but you don't ask.

Laid-off employees are outcasts. Their former coworkers may not speak to them at all. Embarrassment is one reason. Guilt over having ''survived'' is another. Fear of catching the disease is still another. Concern over appearing disloyal to the company is another.

If former coworkers do continue the relationship, they rarely ask for advice. They worry that it would be rude. Perhaps, underneath, they don't believe that someone who has been laid off has much to offer. They are much more comfortable if they can find a reason, real or imaginary, to explain why that person was let go. It makes them feel less vulnerable if they believe the layoff was a rational act or a reasonable consequence of the person's behavior.

The unemployed may be so devastated by their job loss that they consider suicide. It may be very difficult for people who have lost their jobs to talk about the loss and the emotional roller-coaster ride that accompanies it. The more their self-esteem has been based on their job, the more shaken they are by job loss. They may have a hard time—even years later—making sense of their experience and conveying that experience to others.

So, nobody's talking straight. Corporate America is sending mixed and confusing messages. "Survivors" are reluctant to talk to people who have experienced job loss. People who have been laid off are so deeply affected that they have trouble talking about it. The result is that few workers have developed strategies for fireproofing their careers.

That's why we wrote this book. Let's bring the topic of career security out into the open.

Rate Your Readiness

To assess your strengths and weaknesses as you begin to use this book, take the following quiz. As you score yourself, you may find that you need to focus only on a couple of the five strategies in chapters 6 through 10. Perhaps you may want to read and think about all of the ideas in the book. Six months from now, take this quiz again to check your progress toward building a more secure career for yourself.

What's Your Career Security Profile?

Taking the Quiz: Read each statement. Then, circle Y for yes or N for no. At the end of this quiz, you'll find instructions for assessing your career security.

Y N 1. I know exactly how much my essential bills total and have enough money (easily accessible) to take care of them for eight months.

Y N 2. I usually introduce myself by telling my skills and accomplishments rather than by giving my title and company affiliation.

Y N 3. I know from observation and experience about how much severance pay I could count on if I were laid off.

Y N 4. I know at least four criteria for assessing the risk of my job situation.

Y N 5. I/we participate in a savings plan or 401(k).

Y N 6. I/we regularly make other investments (stocks, mutual funds, IRAs, retirement, annuities).

Y N 7. I/we have eliminated credit card debt.

Y N 8. I have initiated my attendance at two in-house training programs in the last year.

Y N 9. I have initiated my attendance at two outside training courses within the past year.

Y N 10. I have or am working on an advanced degree or professional/job credential.

Y N 11. I'm highly visible in two professional organizations and attend more than half their meetings.

Y N 12. I'm a member of at least two other organizations (civic, religious, alumni, etc.) and am active in them in a visible way.

Y N 13. I/we have some kind of additional income besides my salary (rental property, stock dividends, teaching, consulting, etc.).

Y N 14. I have a previous career I could go back to if I had to.

Y N 15. I have a significant interest or activity (volunteer, hobby, etc.) that could be developed into a career.

Y N 16. In the last two years, I've learned a new skill that I don't use in my current job.

Y N 17. During the past year, I have taken advantage of some kind of nontraditional education (audiotape course, noncredit, open university course, private coaching, etc.).

Y N 18. I maintain relationships with people at work outside my department who regularly give me valuable information.

Y N 19. I maintain relationships with at least fifty people outside of work who know my capabilities well.

Y N 20. I've been in the same job for less than five years.

Y N 21. I can identify at least one other job in my organization, but outside my present department, for which I could qualify.

Y N 22. I've been in business for myself or have worked in a family business.

Y N 23. I have changed career fields at least once.

Y N 24. I've lost a job due to circumstances beyond my control at least once and found another job at the same or better salary.

Y N 25. I keep track of the economic and technological trends affecting the organization, industry, and profession in which I work.

Y N 26. I have objective reasons to believe that my performance on the job is above average.

Y N 27. I have a spouse who works, and we have *both* benefit plans in force.

Y N 28. I am in excellent health, exercise regularly, do not smoke, and am not overweight.

Y N 29. I've told friends or acquaintances about at least three job openings in the past year.

Y N 30. I've applied for another job within the past two years.

Scoring Yourself: Enter your score for each question. Give yourself twenty points for each Y answer and ten points for each N answer. Add your scores for each of the five categories: Liberate Your Mind, Line Up Your Finances, Learn for Mastery, Lean Out of Specialization, and Link Up with People.

To find your average in each category, divide by the number of questions in that category.

Enter your average score from each category in the Add Averages column and add those numbers to find your grand total score.

Liberate Your Mind

Item	Score
2	_____
4	_____
13	_____
24	_____
25	_____
30	_____

TOTAL _____
AVG. _____

Line Up Your Finances

Item	Score
1	_____
3	_____
5	_____
6	_____
7	_____
27	_____
28	_____

TOTAL _____
AVG. _____

Learn for Mastery

Item	Score
8	_____
9	_____
10	_____
17	_____
20	_____
26	_____

TOTAL _____
AVG. _____

Lean Out of Specialization

Item	Score
14	_____
16	_____
21	_____
22	_____
23	_____

TOTAL _____
AVG. _____

Link Up with People

Item	Score
11	_____
12	_____
15	_____
18	_____
19	_____
29	_____

TOTAL _____
AVG. _____

Add Averages

Your Score	
Liberate	_____
Line Up	_____
Learn	_____
Lean	_____
Link	_____

GRAND TOTAL _____

Interpreting Your Score: Using your grand total score, find the comments that apply to you below.

50–60 You need to work on all categories to improve your career security. Make your plan. Begin to work on several categories simultaneously. You should be able to raise your score significantly by next year.

61–70 There are several categories you need to work on. If you scored below fifteen in the finance category, work on raising your score there immediately. Using the ideas in this book, you'll be able to improve your career security within one year.

71–80 There are a couple of areas you should strengthen. If you scored below 15 in the finance category, work on raising your score there immediately. Employing the five strategies of security, you will be able to protect yourself adequately within six months.

81–90 You'll quickly be able to maximize your career security by taking a few strategic steps. To determine the steps, analyze the questions you answered with an N. Then make a plan to strengthen yourself in those areas.

91–100 You are in excellent shape to flourish, even if your job disappears. Career security is no problem for you. To determine any actions, analyze the questions you answered with an N.

If your score indicates that you need to work on your career security, don't be disheartened. The ideas in this book will help you address your specific deficiencies. If your score indicates that you should not be worried about your career security, don't be too encouraged. As you learn more about the entire topic, you may find that you have more and more doubts about your readiness to be laid off. You may decide that you have overestimated your ability to continue to make a living, even if your job disappears. The ideas in this book will help you determine what, if anything, you need to do to shore up your long-term security. If you are, indeed, well-prepared, you will be even more confident that you have done the right things to cope with whatever the future brings.

Chapter 2

Job Insecurity

Like the Cheshire Cat in Alice in Wonderland, job security vanished . . . slowly. It began to fade in the eighties. Today, its mocking grin lingers, long after the rest of it has disappeared. You may be expecting old-style security to rematerialize. It's not going to.

You know this, of course, at some level of consciousness. You've read the headlines, day after day, as company after company has announced cutbacks. The truth has begun to sink in.

As the Fortune 1000s have slashed nearly two million jobs from their payrolls over the past four years and smaller firms shed another two million positions, you've gotten the news with your breakfast coffee. You've seen announcements of mergers and acquisitions. You know what follows. Consolidations mean personnel redundancies, especially among the staff at headquarters. You've seen bastions of job security like the military, the U.S. Post Office, and AT&T announce downsizings. The thousands of headlines, trumpeting cutbacks in the manufacturing sector and, more recently, in the service sector, have driven the point home again and again: The numbers of people that have been, and still will be, let go are staggering. In 1994, layoffs continued at a rate of more than 2,000 people a business day, nearly the same pace as during the height of the recent recession. Experts now call layoffs "a way of business life."

You know that those headlines are just the tip of the iceberg. The big companies make the front page. Announcements from the lesser-known, medium-size and small companies are bumped back to the business pages or may appear as a going-out-of-business sale or even a bankruptcy listing.

At the same time, government monthly unemployment statistics are no longer buried at the bottom of the business pages. Those numbers have leaped to the front page. If you share a growing mistrust of government, you may be wondering if these statistics, bad as they seem, understate the problem. They do.

The jobless rate measures only those people who are seeking work and not finding it as a percentage of the total labor force: The statistics you read reflect only those people who are receiving unemployment benefits. They don't count the increasing number of jobless people whose unemployment benefits have run out. They don't include discouraged workers who have given up hunting for a job. They don't show people who have taken part-time work because they can't find full-time jobs. They don't communicate the length of time it's taking people to find jobs. They don't tell you how many people have hung out their shingles as consultants, contract workers, or entrepreneurs, but may not be earning enough money to live on.

You may have read that, at the height of late eighties recession, things really weren't so bad. Experts said that this recession (with unemployment some months topping 7 percent) wasn't nearly as severe as the one in the early eighties. But, as the nineties wear on, you wonder. After previous recessions, didn't the economy bounce back? Weren't the folks who had been laid off laid back on? Somehow, you don't think that's going to happen this time.

You're probably aware of another ominous statistic. In a healthy economy, new jobs would be created at a rate of

200,000 a month. That's not happening, and most of the jobs that are being created are low-paying, low-status jobs.

Why? What's really going on?

The Era Beyond Postwar Expansion

U.S. economic leadership went unchallenged from the end of World War II until the eighties. Oh, the economy had its ups and downs, but things evened out and always got back to "normal." However, the changes going on now are neither temporary nor cyclical. Things will never return to "normal." Most of the jobs being lost now will never come back, even when the economy picks up. They are gone forever. During this time of transition—some have called it a brutal transition—we will see structural changes in the nature of work, in the style and shape of organizations, in the types of industries that flourish, and in the economy, not only in the U.S. but all over the world.

The nation's foremost economists predict that layoffs won't be over soon. One-fourth of the white-collar workforce could still be laid off, says the head of one prominent outplacement firm. Another expert says that there are one and a half managers for every management job, a statistic that indicates that one-third of all managers may still be at risk. In 1994, the focus shifted to the service sector where restructuring is predicted to last at least a decade.

The Vulnerable Middle

Economic vulnerability is a new notion for white-collar workers, whose careers have been built on their bedrock belief in job security. We always thought our education and expertise would immunize us against economic ills, that a bachelor's degree made us bulletproof, and that positive performance appraisals would protect us. The longer we held jobs, the more we were lulled into a false feeling of entitlement. But the rules have changed, and the more things change, the more desperately we cling to the convictions of the past like these:

- A college degree is the ticket to a good life.
- I will be better off, financially, than my parents.
- If I'm loyal and do a good job, I can work for this company until I retire.
- My company values my expertise and experience.
- My company values the ''institutional memory'' of people like me who have been around for a long time and know the company's history and traditions.
- I'm over forty, so I'm protected because of my age.
- When I retire, I trust that I'll still be taken care of by my company and will live comfortably on my pension, which is my reward for my labor and loyalty. Besides, there will be Social Security benefits to help pay the bills.
- My merit raises and excellent performance evaluations protect me from being laid off.
- My job is too important to be eliminated.
- I am too important to be eliminated.
- I've paid my dues and played by the rules, so I'm secure.
- *My* company doesn't lay people off.
- If my company did lay me off, my severance pay would tide me over until I found a job that is equal to or even better than the one I had to leave. Besides, there are unemployment benefits.
- If my company did lay me off, they'd hire an outplacement firm that would find me a good job that is equal to or even better than the one I had to leave.

None of these assumptions is unequivocally true today. As middle managers feel these bedrock beliefs shaking under them, they are in a state of shock. They deny that the changes going on are as pervasive and fundamental as they actually are. Along with denial, however, comes free-floating anxiety and deepening feelings of helplessness as people struggle to deal with permanent uncertainty.

The new vulnerability of white-collar workers isn't just a figment of our imaginations. Middle managers make up only 5 to 8 percent of the workforce, but accounted for 18 percent of the dismissals from since 1988. The blue-collar workforce has always expected temporary layoffs. Those workers have been stunned by the deep, permanent cuts, too. But mid-level workers are the most shocked. This kind of thing simply has never happened to them before. All the old guarantees are gone.

At the same time Mom and Dad are worrying about their jobs, their newly graduated sons and daughters are finding good jobs more and more difficult to come by. More young adults have moved back home with the folks than at any time since the Great Depression.

We're afraid that falling off the career ladder may mean falling out of the middle class. That fear is rooted in reality.

In the early and mid-eighties, 90 percent of laid-off white-collar workers were quickly reemployed at the same or better pay. By the late eighties, only 50 percent were finding new jobs at the same or higher salaries. And by 1994, only 25 percent were able to hang on to their hard-won rung of the ladder; the other 75 percent had slipped down to lower rungs or fallen off the ladder entirely. Landing any new job takes longer now. The average job search for highly paid executives stretches out to eighteen months, three times as long as it took to find a job in the early eighties. In 1993, some 1.75 million people had been out of work at least six months. That figure is 50 percent higher than when the recession bottomed-out in 1991.

Even if you get back into one of the big companies, the glut of managers vying for jobs is depressing salaries. A job that paid $140,000 in 1989 may now pay only $118,000. A typical salary in marketing and sales has slid from $85,000 to $76,000. Many people have taken lower-paying jobs with smaller companies. If you were an executive with a large company who made $240,000, you could expect your salary at a small company to be only $85,000 and your benefits to shrink by 25 percent.

The average stay in a job is now only three and a half years for white-collar workers. Young people entering the workforce can expect to have thirteen different jobs during their careers. Note that many companies offer pensions only to people who have been there for five to seven years. Small companies sometimes offer no pensions at all. Even more frightening is the fact that as mid-level workers move in droves to smaller companies, they may find, if they are laid off from those jobs, that their unemployment is not cushioned by any severance pay at all. Although small businesses are touted as the job creation engines of the future, they can't make up for the cuts made by the giants of American industry. It's a myth that small employers offer more opportunities and increased job security. Small business failures have doubled in the nineties. Only 4 percent of companies with fewer than 100 employee are fast-growing, they account for 70 percent of all new jobs.

The Changes That Are Changing Everything

To blame unemployment on the economy is to make simple what is complex. To understand what's really going on, we must consider a confluence of changes that is restructuring our economic system.

New Types of Industries

What businesses are we in? American industry isn't what it used to be. The shifts are dramatic: from heavy manufacturing to high tech and service, from the hired hand to the hired head, from the Industrial Age to the Information Age, from cars to computer chips. This one statistic says a lot: The computer industry did $150 billion worth of business in 1991—three times that of the auto industry. The switch to high-tech industries means that, because of automation, fewer workers are needed to produce goods. In the growing service industries, more people are needed, but many jobs are low-paying.

New Management Ideas

How should organizations be run? The old hierarchical models are disappearing as companies push responsibility toward people at the bottom of the pyramid. New management styles reduce the need for middle managers. Empowered workers need less supervision. Quality teams find and solve problems without the help of managers. Self-managed work teams don't need layers of managers. Organizations are ferreting out redundant operations and functions as they streamline work processes. Reengineering encourages companies to rethink their work flow, to improve their training and technologies, and, ultimately, to do the same work with 25 to 50 percent fewer workers.

New Sizes of Organizations

How big should companies be? Big companies are still getting bigger. During the eighties, there was an average of thirteen mergers and acquisitions for every business day. In 1993, consolidation continued: Deal-making totaled more than $250 billion. One consequence of these financial maneuvers is high corporate debt. To pay for their buying sprees, organizations are often forced to look for ways to cut costs. The easiest and quickest way to cut costs is to cut people.

New Shapes for Organizations

What does an ideal organization look like? Corporate pyramids are collapsing into pancakes as the the middle layers are being eliminated. Restructuring has become a continuous process. The chain-of-command model, adopted from the church and the military, is dematerializing into fragments that, like colored chips in a kaleidoscope, figure and reconfigure into temporary patterns. Sears Tower no longer symbolizes the ideal corporate headquarters. Concrete fortresses are becoming will-o'-the-wisp concepts, corporations in name only. In the new movie production company model, skilled individuals and groups combine briefly to accomplish goals, then disband.

New Relationships with Employees

What's an employee? Full-time, permanent jobs are disappearing. Looking back to the mid-eighties, Robert Reich, Secretary of Labor, has identified a four-step process that is eliminating the traditional ties between employees and organizations:

Step 1. Reduce benefits for lower-tier workers.
Step 2. Lay off middle management.
Step 3. Reduce benefits for all employees.
Step 4. Contract work out.

Employee-employer bonds are loosening as companies depend more on out-timers, part-timers, and short-timers.

Out-timers: Work in areas such as accounting, benefits, public relations, personnel, food services, maintenance, security, data processing, and engineering is being contracted to outside sources. Outsourcing is accomplished by permanently shifting functions that used to be handled by employees on the *inside* to suppliers on the *outside.*

Outside companies usually pay lower wages and offer fewer benefits for low-skill areas, such as security, so the organization's cost of obtaining those services drops. However, in the high-skill areas, such as computer services, the advantage to the organization may not be price but specialization, technology, and state-of-the-art knowledge. Outsources often pay as well or even better than the companies that use these highly skilled people—migrant managers and professionals with portfolios—who sell their brainpower on the open market.

Individuals also provide expertise on a contract basis. They may be well-paid, but they rarely enjoy any benefits at all. Also, when their contracts end, these workers are not eligible for unemployment.

Part-timers: It's possible that more Americans now work at McDonald's fast-food restaurants than work for General Motors. (McDonald's doesn't know exactly how may people are employed in all its franchised restaurants.) It is true, however, that McDonald's restaurants, like many organizations in the service sector, hire mostly part-time workers. Two-fifths of all jobs in the U.S. are now temporary or part-time. That figure is projected to rise to one-half of all jobs by the turn of the century. As former full-time workers take part-time jobs—sometimes several jobs—to make ends meet, underemployment is the result. People want full-time work but can't find it. This kind of underemployment may be as devastating to middle-class workers as unemployment. Ninety percent of jobs created by companies in February 1993 were part-time jobs, taken by people who wanted to work full-time. Hiring part-timers allowed U.S. employers to cut the nation's $2.6 billion payroll costs by as much as $800 million in 1993 alone.

Short-timers: Temporary workers have tripled over the last decade. The temporary agency, Manpower Inc., with 560,000 workers, was by 1993 the largest private employer in U.S. The growing numbers of temps are the result of accordion management—the practice of expanding or shrinking the workforce to suit business conditions. For businesses, hiring temps has many advantages. Existing outside the system of worker-management relationships and expectations, temporary workers aren't protected by many government requirements, such as equal employment opportunity laws and safety regulations. Temps are easy to get rid of at a moment's notice. Temps don't have to be trained. Businesses use interim assignments as a time to test drive prospective hires, as a way to audition workers for the dwindling number of coveted permanent posts.

A long list of derogatory terms defines the temps' second-class status. Permanent workers are called *core;* temporary workers are dubbed *noncore.* They're referred to as disposable, peripheral, just-in-time (or kanban). They're called short-timers, per-diem workers, leased employees, extras, supplementals, contractors, contingent workers, throwaway workers, and mercenaries. They're called disposable workers and their jobs are also disposable.

One sure way to increase productivity statistics is to reduce headcount, and increasing productivity is a long-standing corporate goal. The invisible hands of contingent workers contribute to organizational output, but productivity statistics don't count their contributions.

There is no evidence to suggest that these trends—practices that tear away the bonds between employers and employees—will change any time soon. One-fourth of all jobs created during the recovery have been temporary, an unprecedented statistic.

New Competition

Who can do it best and cheapest? Competition, both global and domestic, is a complicated, fast-moving constellation of changes. The global economy pits U.S. companies against foreign rivals. Tough competition from the Far East and Europe has compelled American business to reexamine its fundamental philosophies. In some arenas, competition is a fact of life; in others, it's a future threat. Still dominating the world's aerospace industry, U.S. aerospace companies are preparing for long-term international competition.

Product Competition: Who builds better mousetraps? U.S. auto manufacturers have improved their products and are giving Japanese car manufacturers a run for their money. However, they still haven't overtaken Japan's auto leaders who drove away with a big chunk of the American auto business in the seventies.

Wage Competition: People costs are 30 to 80 percent of a company's general and administrative costs. It's no wonder that executives look at the largest piece of the cost pie and start cutting there. In the U.S., salaries account for 26.6 percent of manufacturing costs compared to 21.6 percent in Germany and only 17.9 percent in Japan. In Latin America and Asia, workers toil all day to earn what American workers make in an hour. Low-priced workers in factories in Brazil or Taiwan churn out goods. As American consumers buy those goods, they put themselves out of work. In global competition, American workers are sure to lose because companies will farm out work to the cheapest labor. American workers' wages are in competition with wages around the world. The global market price for employees affects our wage structures.

Industry Competition: In the U.S., there are too many firms in such industries as retailing and real estate, chasing too few customers. Retail store square footage, for example, has grown tenfold in the last ten years, while population growth has been puny.

Job Competition: Baby boomers, born between the mid-forties and the mid-sixties, are a demographic bulge, fast settling into the mid-management, mid-career stage of midlife. More than 50 million over-the-hill boomers are competing in unprecedented numbers for a shrinking number of jobs. Many have fallen victim to their own success. As they climbed up the ladder to higher and higher layers of management, garnering automatic annual raises and promotions, they have priced themselves out of the job market.

New Technologies

Why not get a machine to do the job? Automated teller machines cut into the numbers of bank tellers. Optical character readers displace typists and data entry clerks. Voice mail technology thins the ranks of receptionists. Rule of thumb: When technology takes over a high-skill function, the result is a low-skill job. Simultaneously, automation is reducing the need for the report writing, monitoring, and statistic compiling that used to be part of almost every middle manager's job description. Computers also increase the number of employees a manager can manage. Management theory used to say that one supervisor could handle seven employees; now the number of people that one manager is expected to supervise has shot up to thirty and is still rising.

People look to the service sector to provide new jobs to replace those lost in manufacturing. Ironically, service businesses, the only area in which jobs are increasing, will be the next prime target for downsizing, as new labor-cutting technologies displace workers.

New Government Initiatives

How much government is good? Current political priorities are resulting in short-term job losses. Uncertainty about changing laws and regulations discourages companies from hiring.

Trimming the National Debt: Curtailing government spending is high on the public agenda. However, many of the deepest cuts proposed have been temporarily avoided as advocates of targeted areas fight to keep pet projects. The debt is a sword hanging over the heads of all American workers.

Streamlining Government: Statistics show that government work—local, state, and federal—is one of the fastest growing occupations in the U.S. More than 18.8 million people derive their paychecks from some level of government. Nonetheless, public sentiment favors making government smaller and more efficient.

Creating a National Health System: The health care industry anticipates legislation that will increase competition and put caps on prices. Nearly 60 percent of the nation's employers expect the health care reform initiative to hurt the economy. They say it will put too much of a burden on companies that are required to pay the bulk of medical insurance costs for their employees.

Cutting the Defense Budget: The end of the Cold War has encouraged Congress to make its first real cuts in defense spending since World War II. Because the defense industry is so large and employs so many people, retrenching in that sector cascades through the economy. Closing a base affects businesses throughout the entire community. Housing prices plunge, sales tax revenues fall, and the dry cleaner who used to spiff up all those uniforms closes his doors forever. One outplacement firm estimates that two-thirds of the job cuts in the defense sector are still to come.

Raising Taxes: When increased profitability only brings new and heavier taxes, businesses have no incentive to expand. Since demand for goods and services isn't strong enough to offset higher taxes, companies say they have to cut costs to maintain profitability.

Regulating for the Social Good: New environmental regulations, updated civil rights legislation, the Americans with Disabilities Act, and the Family and Medical Leave Act, to single out just a few items from a long list, dampen the hiring enthusiasm of American businesses. There's evidence that some companies make a calculated decision to forgo growth so that they don't hit the fifty-employee mark, at which point more regulatory controls kick in. Continual lobbying for minimum wage increases also exerts downward pressures. Anything that increases the cost of labor will depress the demand for labor to some degree. We may applaud the goals of regulatory activism, but its effect may be to stifle business.

Deregulating for the Social Good: The freeing up of areas such as telecommunications and banking has resulted in consolidation within these industries. Massive deregulatory moves, begun in the mid-eighties, are now being aided and abetted by automation, especially in such industries as communications and banking. The chubby communications utilities are still slimming down. Meanwhile, banks, thrown into competition with a multitude of financial service institutions, must continue to reduce their workforces.

New Worries on the Part of Consumers

Where is it all going to end? That's what consumers are wondering. Consumer buying of goods and services accounts for two-thirds of the gross domestic product. When great numbers of consumers get scared about their ability to maintain their earning power, they hold off and cut back on spending. Income tax increases leave fewer dollars for discretionary spending. It's a vicious cycle. Employers reduce costs by laying off employees or by not hiring. Fear increases and confidence wanes among workers. They become more reluctant consumers and choosier when they do buy. This caution renews the pressure on companies to reduce prices. These companies lay off more people, thus spreading more fear of firing.

The Dumb Side of Downsizing

Has downsizing become a measure of macho management? Some researchers and observers of the phenomenon think so. Commentators accuse executives of becoming addicted to layoffs. Once a few companies in an industry downsize, others follow, and copycat layoffs sweep through that industry. Executives bow to peer pressure and play follow the leader.

With all that has been said and written about the trend toward softer management styles, it's amazing that tough guy management is still so admired. Executives may feel they must demonstrate their toughness by bragging about how many people they have laid off recently.

The reasoning on Executive Row goes like this. If the problem is profitability, we should cut payroll. If we cut payroll, we can show increased earnings in the next quarterly financial report. If our earnings numbers rise, so will our stock price. If our stock price goes up, directors and investors will be pleased. If we make them happy, we will be rewarded.

The benefits of this scenario are not substantiated by research. New evidence indicates that downsizing doesn't cure what ails companies. "Economic benefits, such as lower expenses ratios, higher profits, increased return-on-investment, and boosted stock prices" fail to materialize, says Dr. Wayne Cascio, a professor at the University of Colorado at Denver who has studied the consequences of downsizing. Layoffs may eliminate a competitive disadvantage, but may not create a competitive advantage for the future.

Nonetheless, lopping people off the payroll has become a knee-jerk strategy, the number one way to cut costs. Layoffs have become the first resort, not the last.

Norm, who works for a pharmaceutical company, remembers a task force that met several years ago to figure out all the steps the company would take to avoid handing out pink slips. The group came up with a list of more than 100 cost-cutting strategies that would be implemented before the company would resort to a layoff. Then the company merged with another firm whose culture was not so averse to laying off employees. The company's customers changed as more and more doctors joined health care organizations that took responsibility for ordering drugs. Because there was no longer any need to call on individual doctors, fewer salespeople were needed. Norm found himself responsible for letting 600 people go. Although he originally approached the task with many reservations left over from his immersion in the old, no-layoff culture, he eventually convinced himself that reducing headcount was the right thing to do. Right or wrong, the company had moved layoffs from the bottom to the top of its list of cure-alls.

In half the companies surveyed for one study, there wasn't much management going on at all. These companies were flying by the seat of their pants, laying people off just to deal with the crisis of the moment, desperately flailing about to get costs down and profits up. Amazingly, many executives reached for the ax, even when high costs were not the problem. Only 1 percent of the companies studied assigned people to work creatively on anticipating change and planning for the future. One inescapable conclusion is that, if companies managed better and learned how to anticipate changes, hundreds of thousands of layoffs might be avoided.

Cascio also found that expected organizational benefits, such as lower overhead, smoother communications, greater entrepreneurship, and increased productivity fail to develop after a downsizing. Instead, the most certain impact of downsizing is a nosedive in employee morale: a deep sense of betrayal, increased disillusionment, and rampant cynicism. With these kinds of negative worker attitudes, productivity is almost certain to deteriorate.

Managers often end up hiring new workers to do the very jobs that the previous layoff had trimmed away as fat. One expert says half of all excess jobs are refilled within one year of being eliminated. Often, however, these replacement workers are less experienced, cheaper employees. Sometimes the company hires back the pink-slipped workers as part-timers without benefits, and sometimes the company contracts with outside companies or individuals to get the work done. Occasionally, such shenanigans work to the employee's benefit. One bookkeeper who was making nine dollars an hour was laid off, then called back at a contract worker's salary of forty-two dollars an hour.

When organizations play this game, it's quite possible to show a decline in headcount while real labor expenses rise. Only full-time, permanent workers are paid from the official payroll; the wages of part-timers and out-timers are buried in nonpayroll budgets.

Here are the terrible truths about downsizing:

- Layoffs aren't always rational, well-thought-out responses to business situations.

- They rarely have the desired results.
- They always severely damage morale.
- They often lead to higher-cost solutions in the long run.
- They almost never fix the problems.

Assess Your Situation

To determine the risk level of your particular job, look at your industry, your company, your geographic location, your job type, your own job, and your personal attributes and assets. Consider the questions under each heading to get a sense of how nervous you should be about your current job security and how imperative it is that you get cracking to implement the strategies in chapters 6 through 10.

Your Industry

- Have there been layoffs in other companies in your industry? (Layoffs are catching; once one company downsizes, others will copy.)
- Are there mergers or acquisitions going on in your industry? (Consolidation means job redundancy.)
- Are there government initiatives under way that might affect your industry? (Uncertainty about future policies can scare companies into cost-cutting.)
- Did your industry grow fat in the eighties? Does it need to slim down?
- What's the level of competition? (In some industries, too many companies are fighting over too few customers.)
- Where is competition coming from? What's the basis of the competitive threat? Wage competition? Product competition?
- Is your industry emerging and growing? Has it matured? Is it in a maintenance mode? Is it over the hill? Is it on the edge of obsolescence?
- What are the demographics? Is your industry's customer base expanding, leveling off, or declining?
- How automated is your industry? What new technologies are coming down the pike?

If you don't know the answers to these questions, read trade journals, financial publications, comments and reports by financial analysts, and books and newsletters on trends, such as *The Popcorn Report: On the Future of Your Company, Your World, Your Life* by Faith Popcorn, and *John Naisbitt's Trend Letter.* Attend industry conferences or get audiotapes of key speakers to find out what industry leaders are saying. Tune into the big picture. There's no such thing as a safe industry anymore.

Your Company

- What are your executives saying or not saying?
- What were your company's profits last year? (Most employees don't know the answer to this simple question.)
- How satisfied are executives and stockholders about the level of profitability? What are your company's expectations? (At one company, people were used to double-digit increases every year. Amazingly, when profit growth slowed to single-digit increases, the company decided it had to downsize. In that company, satisfaction with the level of profitability was more important than actual numbers.)
- How does your company's market share compare with that of your competitors? Is your share expanding or contracting?
- How did your unit or division do?
- Did the particular product or service you are most closely connected with do well or poorly?
- In your industry, is your company of medium size? (Mid-size organizations are the most at risk.)
- How much automation has gone on in your organization? Is there more to come?
- How many layers of management are there? (Could your company compress ten layers into six or even four?)
- Does your company depend on business from other organizations that are going through cutbacks?
- How do your company's overhead costs compare with those of your domestic and international rivals?
- What's the cash flow picture? What portion of earnings is going to repay debt?

- What do financial analysts say about your company?
- Has your company downsized already? (You may have heard that lightning doesn't strike twice in the same spot. Not true. A company that has downsized once will likely do it again. Ongoing staff reductions may become part of the corporate culture.)
- Has your company already tried other cost-cutting measures?
- Has your company offered an early retirement program?
- Who is being hired? What talents and skills are most valued now? Are you getting any hints about what will be valued in the future? Who is getting promoted? What degrees and abilities do new hires have? How old are they?

Your Job Type

- Are you a member of any group likely to be affected by a downsizing? ("Human resources people are like tree surgeons," someone once said. "Once the damaged limb is gone, they are, too.")
- Could the kind of work you do be outsourced? (A growing trend is to rent professionals, such as lawyers or accountants, from an agency.)
- Could another department do the work that your department does?
- Is your job a line job or a staff job? (Staff jobs are less secure.)
- Do you work in a headquarters group? (Headquarters personnel are often perceived as pure overhead.)
- Is there a way to automate much of what you do?
- Is your main responsibility to filter or compile information? Is it to monitor, check, or inspect? (Look out!)
- Are you a manager who manages managers?
- If your function doesn't serve customers directly, how directly does the area you serve contribute to the bottom line?

Your Own Job

- How enthusiastic was your boss about your performance in your last evaluation?
- How did your last raise compare with the raises of your

colleagues in your department?

- How visible are you? Do the movers and shakers know who you are?
- Can you substantiate your direct contribution to the bottom line? (The farther you get away from the customer, the more difficult it is to justify your salary in a crunch.)
- Could your job be done by a contractor or consultant?
- Have you been in your present position more than three years? (With the average job tenure shrinking to only three and a half years, if you've been in your job longer, you may be on borrowed time.)
- If your organization has a point system for ranking jobs, do you know how many points your job has? (After Doris was laid off, she found out that if her job had been ranked one point higher, she would have been eligible for twice the severance pay she received.)
- Is there someone else in your department in a lower salary range who could do your job?
- Are you violating any of the "rules" in your corporate culture? (Homer spent a lot of time on the job with volunteer activities. After a merger, the culture changed and volunteering was no longer a valued activity, but he continued his heavy involvement. Good-bye, Homer.)
- Has your office been moved to the basement or to a trailer behind the building?

Your Geographic Location

- How healthy is the economy in the city and region where your headquarters is located? Where are key units of the company located? Are they being affected by local or regional layoffs in other industries?
- Is your company located in an area with a diversified economy? (The safest locations are ones with several employers in different industries who hire people with your expertise.)
- Has a dominant employer in the region downsized? (In March 1993, IBM laid off 8,900 workers in the Hudson Valley region of New York. Economists predicted that, for every person laid off by IBM, an additional one and a half

to two jobs in the region would disappear.)

- What job hunting and career counseling services and support organizations are available in your city?
- How are housing prices holding up in your location? (In some parts of the country, housing values have declined so much that many people owe more on their mortgages than their homes are worth on the market.)

Your Personal Attributes and Assets

- How's your morale? (Research indicates that "survivors" of layoffs become narrow-minded, self-absorbed and risk-averse. How's your attitude?)
- Are you over forty? (Older workers may have received automatic salary increases for many years, making them prime candidates to be replaced by younger, cheaper workers.)
- Are your credentials and education comparable to or better than those of new hires and others in your work group?
- Are you married to a person who has a well-paid job of a different type in a different company in a different industry? (Your spouse is a vital part of your long-term career security. Differentiation makes you less vulnerable. Stories abound of spouses whose woes were doubled when they were laid off at the same time.)
- How mobile are you? Could you move if you had to?

Watch for the Warning Signs

Part of your risk assessment must be to look around you and make sense of what you see. In a cartoon, a man is sitting at his desk. Behind him on his office wall, scrawled like graffiti, are the messages, "Get out, you loser" and "You're a bum." The caption reads, "Near the end, Lloyd could read the writing on the wall."

Many people miss the messages. Be observant. Look for these signs:

- Vacant jobs are being left unfilled.
- There has been an increase in the number of new hires. (Em-

ployees at a telecommunications company were confused: The company was downsizing and offering early outs, but it was still hiring young people. Employees figured that either management was crazy, or everything was okay because the company was still hiring. One person who was later laid off said, "We should have seen that the new, younger people cost the company less. We also should have noticed which areas were growing. Most of those new employees were going into the overseas divisions.")

- Your company has instituted a hiring freeze.
- Rumors about your company offering an early retirement program are circulating.
- Work hours have been reduced. (In some organizations every employee at every level has been told to take a day or several days off without pay.)
- Overtime is prohibited.
- Field offices are being closed or consolidated.
- The company has stepped up cross training, so one person knows how to do more than one job and could, in fact, do the jobs of several other people.
- A new top management team has been brought in.
- Your boss is talking about looking for another job or retiring.
- Your boss's boss has left or been laid off.
- You have a new boss.
- Expense checks or commission checks are late.
- Projects are being put on hold.
- The company has slashed its advertising budget.
- Major purchases have been postponed or canceled.
- Another department has started to do work similar to that done in your department.
- The annual Christmas party or traditional summer picnic has been canceled.
- The annual departmental or company-wide planning retreat has been postponed.
- Your company has started a library of career books or opened a career center. (One publisher says he knows when a company is planning a layoff because he gets an order for an entire library of career planning books.)

- The product or service you are most closely associated with has bombed in the marketplace.
- You are no longer invited to the meetings you used to attend.
- Your phone calls are not returned promptly.
- Your name has been dropped from the routing slip for important memos.
- Your calendar for the next six months looks rather bare.
- The maintenance crew has stopped watering your plants.
- Your request to have your office painted has been denied.

If you understand the reasons behind job insecurity, if you take the time to carefully assess your own situation, and if you tune in to the warning signs, you will be more prepared to acknowledge the risks you face right now.

Chapter 3

More Than a Paycheck

Work provides more than a salary. What you do determines how you view yourself—your self-concept, your self-confidence, your self-image, your self-worth, your self-esteem. It also influences how others view you—your identity, your status, your station in life.

The belief that you are your job title is reinforced every day.

At a dinner party, Alexa noticed a man asking, "What do you do?" of the person across the table. When he replied, "I'm a teacher," the man smiled politely, turned away, and asked the same question of a young woman seated next to him. She replied, "I'm an administrator." Again, the man moved on, leaving the distinct impression that those jobs did not qualify as interesting or impressive.

Amused, Alexa got ready to answer when the man at last turned to her. "I'm a brain surgeon," she lied. Immediately, the man became attentive, excited, and interested.

Sad, but true.

The first thing we ask when we meet people is the question: "What do you do?" Then we pigeonhole them as soon as they give us the answer. People's contributions to society gain less respect than the checks they receive on payday. We may be painfully aware that teachers deserve more respect as well as more pay, but we treat teachers as if they have lower status than, say, attorneys.

The pecking order is well-established and even acknowledged by people as they introduce themselves. In recent years, women have been admonished, "Don't say, 'I'm just a housewife' or 'I'm just a secretary.' " But the women who introduce themselves that way do so because they know that society places little importance on their contributions.

In the past, working women have sometimes dismissed other women who don't work as unimportant and uninteresting. Now there's grudging acceptance that women who stay at home certainly do labor, and the correctly worded question to ask a woman is, "Do you work outside the home?"

Wives have always enjoyed the status accorded to their husbands. More recently, husbands also have been able to gain points for their wives' success.

Parents bask in the reflected glory of their offsprings' status, saying with pride, "My son, the doctor . . ." Kids as young as grade schoolers feel intense pressure to select the right careers. Nobody thinks it's cute when a sixteen-year-old says he wants to be a fireman.

Children desperately try to meet their parents' expectations. Dov, who is thirty-three, says, "I'm a social worker." Immediately, he follows that information with a confession. "My parents are very disappointed that I'm not doing something important," he says. "I thought maybe I could satisfy them by making money. I own some property and make a great deal of money from my investments, but they still don't respect me." He's halfheartedly working on a master's degree in business management. "I'm making one more attempt to impress my parents," he explains.

The higher you go on the organization chart, the more you are admired. At work, the desire to climb the ladder often overshadows people's desire to do the business of the business. People seem less concerned about profits and productivity than about their position and the perks, privilege, prestige, and pay that go along with higher-status jobs.

Titles are inflated to gain status. A secretary is elevated to assistant to the president. An animal caretaker at the zoo's monkey house refers to himself as a primate nutrition specialist.

And so it goes: In American society, you are what you do.

Fireproofing your career is not only a matter of taking action to secure your career if your job disappears. In a society that worships job titles and six-figure incomes, it's also about protecting your sense of self-worth.

If you lose your job, how will you answer the question, "What do you do?" If your sense of self is too tied to your employment status, unemployment can be devastating. Your feeling of self-worth can be stripped away the moment you are laid off unless you free yourself from equating work with worth.

"I had become my work. I defined myself as someone who did that job at that place," remembers Carin. She remembers, too, how she referred to her company as "they" when she started working there and how quickly she began to say "we," as she became one with the organization.

The pleasure you take in introducing yourself by your title and organizational affiliation is an indicator of your dependency on that relationship to provide your self-esteem. Think about how you feel as you tell what you do. Do you puff up with pride as you mention your title? Are you aware of being a member of an elite group as you name your employer? Can you almost see yourself shoot up in your listener's estimation as you identify yourself by your job?

These feelings are danger signals.

Our Work Is Our Worth

Where do we get the idea that our success at work is the measure of our worth as a human being? This idea is imbedded in our cultural history.

In Europe in the Middle Ages, work wasn't very important. The dominant cultural institution of the times, the Roman Catholic Church, taught that people should live simply. Prayer, meditation, contemplation, and doing penance for one's sins in preparation for life after death were much more important than work. Poverty was a virtue. Matthew 19:24 in the Bible provided an oft-quoted scriptural reference: "It is easier for a camel to go through the eye of a needle, than for a rich man to enter into the kingdom of God."

With the Protestant Reformation came new ideas about work. Martin Luther taught that it was good to pursue worldly wealth and success. John Calvin took that idea farther, creating the theory of predestination. That theory set forth the notion that God either saved or damned you at birth. There was nothing you could do to change your fate and no way of knowing which group you belonged to. Understandably, that uncertainty made people nervous. They desperately wanted to know which group they'd been assigned to.

Calvin's followers came up with a sign of salvation. They decided that the *electi,* those favored by God, could be recognized by their success. If you were not successful and did not amass worldly goods, God obviously was not smiling on you. If you did become wealthy, God most certainly was beaming. Your wealth symbolized your salvation.

Because of these ideas, the Protestants valued and emphasized such traits as self-discipline, thrift, ambition, diligence, and perseverance. Anything that wasted time, on the other hand, even spending time in church and praying, was considered a vice. The Protestants were not content to wait for God to drop success in their laps; they believed the Lord helps those who help themselves.

These ideas live today, deep in the American psyche. Most of us judge our worth and the worth of other people by material success. The decade of the eighties with its motto, "The one with the most toys wins," may have been the pinnacle of materialism.

Because they lack a job and are therefore cut off from amassing wealth, the symbol of God's blessing, people who are out of work are devalued. We may even believe that people who have lost their jobs deserve their fate. It's comforting to think that way. Believing that life is just, we think that the capable—like ourselves—couldn't possibly be laid off. If you work hard to get a college education and perform well on the job, you will be safe, we think. That's not true, of course, in today's economy where the sword falls indiscriminately. Restructurings, mergers, downsizings, bankruptcies, and plant closings hit excellent as well as mediocre performers. This reality has shocked millions of laid-off workers.

"Your pride goes to pot when you are laid off," says Brian. He believes that, instead of attributing job loss to the economy, many people tend to blame themselves. "People feel full of self-blame and shame," he says, "as if their predicament is their fault."

If your sense of self-worth is derived exclusively or even primarily from your work, losing your job means losing your value as a human being.

Work and Self-esteem

What is self-esteem? Psychologists have been asking that question for thirty years and are far from reaching a consensus on a simple definition. Dr. Nathaniel Branden, who has written and spoken on the topic for three decades, defines self-esteem this way:

- Confidence in your ability to think
- Confidence in your ability to cope with the challenges of life
- Confidence in your right to be happy

He goes on to say that self-esteem also is "the feeling of being worthy, deserving, entitled to assert our needs and wants and to enjoy the fruits of our efforts."

With high self-esteem, you have an "immune system of consciousness," Branden believes. This protective system strengthens you to face the ups and downs of living. Without high self-esteem, you lack resilience, the ability to bounce back when life gets tough.

In his most recent book, *The Six Pillars of Self-esteem,* Branden says to strengthen self-esteem, you must

- Live consciously
- Accept yourself
- Take responsibility for yourself
- Express and assert yourself
- Have a purpose
- Practice integrity

These behaviors have a sort of chicken or the egg relationship with self-esteem: they both encourage it and express it.

Notice that self-esteem comes from inside; it is not based on external trappings, like title or income, nor is it based on other people's assessment of your worth. What happens if we allow our work to determine our level of self-esteem? Branden warns against this: "To tie our self-esteem to any factor outside our . . . control . . . is to invite anguish."

Yet we do just that. We say to ourselves, "I work therefore I am."

The Voice in Your Head

After Judi was laid off, she heard the voice in her head. It was louder than usual and persistent: "In some dark place inside my mind there was a voice that said over and over again: 'You are worthless. You deserved this.' "

It's natural to doubt your abilities if you are laid off, but beating up on yourself is detrimental to getting on with your life.

Inside your head is a voice that talks to you constantly. Stop reading, right now, and listen to that voice. Hear it? Unfortunately, much of what it says to us is negative. One researcher estimates that as much as 77 percent of what we say to ourselves about ourselves can be classified as self-rejecting. As you drive to work, for example, your voice commands the air waves of your mind, worrying and criticizing:

"You idiot, you forgot to call Jim back."

"Why didn't you sell those stocks earlier? You'll never learn."

You can take charge of that negative voice and refuse to

allow it to undermine you now, as you work toward fireproofing your career, or later, if you go through the experience of losing your job. Managing that voice—changing it from a critic that sabotages you to a coach that supports you—may not increase your self-esteem, but taking charge of what you say to yourself can prevent you from succumbing to the self-battering that is detrimental to your self-confidence, just when you need that self-confidence the most.

Your mind believes what it hears about you. If a child is told over and over that he's clumsy, chances are very good that even the most well-coordinated kid will eventually begin to fall all over himself. Your critic replays, builds on, and expands on every negative comment that's ever been directed your way.

Your critic comments about what you have or haven't done in the past and what you will or won't do in the future. It gives you bad reviews and bad previews. Your critic is prosecuting attorney, judge, and jury, and the verdict is always "Guilty!"

We all live with our heads full of two kinds of "truths" about ourselves: facts and fictions. Facts are verifiable statements, like

- "I'm thirty-nine years old."
- "I weight 142 pounds."
- "I graduated from the University of Chicago."

We also tell ourselves a lot of fictions. These fictions are both negative or positive judgments you make about yourself, like

- "I'm no good with numbers."
- "I'm scared of flying."
- "I'm not creative."

Or

- "I'm a numbers person."
- "I'm not scared of anything."
- "I'm creative."

You may or may not be able to verify these judgments. Even if they're totally fictitious, you act as if they're true. You tell other people these "truths" and get them to believe and buy into your fictional reality.

Take Charge of How You Talk to Yourself

Change your "I cant's," your "I shoulds," your "I'm going to try tos," and your "I want tos" into positive, personal, perfect, and passionate affirmations of your ability to flourish in your career.

The I Can'ts: When you say, "I can't . . ." to yourself, your brain hears, "I accept this limitation in myself." You might say, for example, "I just can't walk up to a perfect stranger and start talking at a networking event."

The I Shoulds: If you say, "I should change careers," there's often another, unspoken corollary that affects your behavior: "I should . . . but I won't," "I should . . . but I'm not going to," "I should . . . but I can't." Saying, "I need to . . ." or "I ought to . . ." has the same negative effect.

The I'm Going to Try Tos: When you say, "I'm going to try to . . . ?" you withhold your total commitment. Trying gives you an out. It allows you to procrastinate, to fiddle, and to fail.

The I Want Tos: When you say, "I want to . . ." that's a wish without a plan. Such statements as these allow you to wander in the foggy land of fantasy.

To take charge of your self-talk, capture your critic. Listen for the voice in your head and write down what it says. Then, rewrite the critical self-talk into coach-talk.

Make your coach's statements

- *Positive.* Don't say, "I do not procrastinate." Avoid the word *not.* Somehow, the brain overlooks that word and hears

"I do procrastinate." So instead, say, "I start tasks quickly."

- *Personal.* Use the word *I* to begin every statement.
- *Perfect.* State your thought as if you have already accomplished the change. Give your brain a picture of yourself after you have completed your change. Don't say, "I will—or I can—get another job." Say, "I take steps every day to increase my chances of finding the perfect job for myself."
- *Passionate.* Use exciting words. Say, "I thrive on . . ." "I love to . . ." or "I enthusiastically pursue . . ." The more emotion your statement generates in you, the faster your mind will find ways to help you accomplish whatever you want to do.

Your mind doesn't like inconsistency. If you tell yourself negative things, your mind helps them come true. If you tell yourself positive things, your mind encourages behavior that leads to your goals.

Use this process to go from critic to coach. First, write down a bunch of negative thoughts. Then, transform them into affirmations. After you have finished writing your positive statements, get some three-by-five-inch index cards. Use one card for each affirmation. Write each statement on a card three times. Make the first two renditions identical. Start the third rendition with the word *You.*

Here's an example of what one of your index cards might say:

> I work every day to implement the survival strategies in my life.
> I work every day to implement the survival strategies in my life.
> You work every day to implement the survival strategies in your life.

The third statement acts like an approving parent and gives you positive strokes.

Read each card ten times a day. If it's difficult for you to take time to do this, record your statements on tape and play the tape as you're getting ready for work, driving in the car, or doing the dishes.

As you read or listen to your statements, "Yes, buts . . ." will come up: "Yes, but my neighbor's been out of work for ten months." Don't let your "Yes, buts . . ." bully you. Keep feeding yourself good thoughts. Feel the emotion and excitement. Allow yourself to believe what you are saying to yourself. Picture yourself doing what your statement says. Reading an affirmative statement silently provides a 10 percent impact. Reading and picturing your statement has a 55 percent impact. But, reading, picturing, and feeling together have a 100 percent impact. Go for the 100 percent.

Whenever your critic says something that makes you feel uncomfortable and incapable of dealing with the possibility of making a job transition, transform that negative statement into an encouraging one that makes you feel capable and strong. Acting as your own coach, say that statement over and over to yourself.

Critic	**Coach**
I'm too old to get another job.	I can use my maturity and experience in many ways to make a living.
I should have changed companies two years ago when I had the chance.	I know how to make the best of all the twists and turns in my career.
I'm going to try to network more often.	I enthusiastically network to build strong, supportive relationships with a wide variety of people.

You'll be amazed at the feelings of well-being and confidence that your coach can give you as you deal with a career change. Belief creates reality, so how you talk to yourself about your ability to cope is a vital step in fireproofing your career. Equally as important are actions that you take now to put work in its place in your life.

Your Work Is Not Your Life

Roberto said, "I'll die if I lose my job." He won't, of course. Neither will you. Your work is not your life. Organizations encourage this kind of thinking when they gobble up more and more hours of your day. It's not uncommon, in today's leaner and meaner workplace, for the organization to demand that people work late every night and then come into the office on Saturdays. When this happens, there is nothing in your life except work.

It may be impossible to resist the demands. Calvin had literally been working eighty-two-hour weeks for six and a half months to complete a special project that showed no signs of winding down. He and his wife had three small children and another on the way. She also had a career. Their family life in a shambles, Calvin finally went to see his boss and said, "I can't continue to work these hours." The boss pointed to a stack of resumes on his desk and replied, "If you don't want to do it, I can find somebody else." Reluctantly, Calvin buckled under to the demands.

One top executive of a major telecommunications firm sent a memo to all employees, the "survivors" of a series of layoffs. It said, in part: "I ask each of you to be introspective about the adequacy of your commitment. . . . Forty-hour work weeks are a relic of the past." With more people out of work, organizations push to get more work out of those who remain.

Sometimes, employees themselves actually contribute to the creation of this mind-set. Fearing for your job security, you may assume that putting in many extra hours of office time will prevent the next downsizing from touching you. Working long hours does not protect your job in a layoff situation.

When entire divisions or functions are eliminated, individual performance counts for nothing.

John remembers his boss coming into his cubicle at 5:30 P.M., night after night, bearing yet another project and saying, "John, I need this tomorrow morning." This kind of situation became routine. Often, however, the projects were ill-conceived—things that didn't need to be done at all when John examined them rationally in the light of day, and the work he'd done the night before usually ended up in the wastebasket before lunch. "It was crazy," he remembers.

Sometimes, there really wasn't any work to do at all, and people simply hung around. A colleague would suggest ordering a pizza. John would say, "I just want to get out of here." The colleague would reply, "Well, it won't look good if we leave before 10 P.M., so we might as well get something to eat."

People who worked for this company actually bought casual clothes—an entire Saturday-at-the-office wardrobe. They not only had to be there and be seen, they had to wear the weekend uniform!

When John was presented with the choice to take either a demotion and a cut in pay or to leave with a severance package, he decided to bail out. "The stress and anxiety weren't worth it. I could feel my life shrinking day by day," he said.

Putting in excessive overtime is dangerous. Working all the time means that

- You have no identity except your work identity.
- You have no friends except your work friends.
- Your relationship with your spouse and family weakens.
- You have no time to spend networking.
- You have no time to spend gaining educational or professional credentials that might enhance your future marketability.
- You have no time to eat properly or exercise regularly.
- You have no time for recreation or significant volunteer work.
- You can't moonlight or run a business on the side.

- You have no time to think about anything except work.
- Most dangerous of all, you make yourself believe that you will be rewarded for your dedication.

In short, you become extremely vulnerable and create a situation in which, if a layoff occurs, you feel the deepest sense of betrayal. ''I gave them 210 percent, and they still laid me off. How could they do this to me?'' is the anguished cry of far too many laid-off workers.

''I lived, ate, and breathed that company,'' remembers Kyle. He especially regrets taking the family on vacation and then missing all the fun as he spent six hours a day on the phone with his office. ''Now that I've been laid off, I can see that I gave too much of myself to the organization.''

In one survey, 43 percent of employees said that their workloads were too large and the demands of the job excessive. Whether your organization demands too much or whether you become a willing collaborator in creating this kind of debilitating workplace environment, you must take a hard look at what you can do to cut your work week back to size. If work takes over your life, you will find it impossible to implement the survival strategies outlined in this book.

Put Work in Its Place

Putting all your eggs in one basket is dangerous. Managers and professionals define their social identities through their occupations more than any other segment of the working population. ''When I lost my job, I didn't know where I fit in the world or who I was,'' says Vincent. ''When my title was taken from me, my life lost its meaning and purpose because I had nothing else.''

Men are more at risk than women when they give too much to their jobs because men typically define themselves more by their jobs and achievements than do women.

Women typically define themselves more by their relationships—wife, mother, friend—than do men, so women's self-concepts are less likely to be tied up in their titles and company affiliations. Women also usually have a larger number of supportive relationships in their lives than men do—relationships that help them cope with change and loss. Because there still is sex discrimination in the workplace, some women have realized that getting ahead may be difficult or even impossible. For that reason, they may have avoided investing themselves as wholeheartedly in their jobs as men have. For all these reasons, women may be less shaken than men if they are laid off.

Whether you are a man or a woman, if you wear more than one hat, if you have more than one identity in life, you will fare far better if and when you are handed a pink slip.

Helen was let go along with 400 other people from her company. As she talked with some of the others, she began to recognize that she was one of only a few who had built a strong identity outside the company. She hadn't realized how much her activities outside of work would bolster her sense of self-worth when she no longer could introduce herself using her title and company.

The same week she was laid off, her first book was accepted by a publisher, so Helen had begun to think of herself as an author. She had been teaching an evening course at a university for four years, so college professor was another of her identities. She had been speaking and presenting workshops on writing for a variety of organizations nationwide, so, speaker and trainer were other hats she wore frequently. Losing her job meant that she lost only one of her several identities.

Immediately after Helen was laid off, when people asked her, "What do you do?" even though she no longer had an organization, she had an answer—in fact, she had several answers.

People who have a variety of relationships and interests and places where they belong are more able to endure job loss without being devastated by it.

In the nineties, people are creating new values as well as multiple identities in order to put work in its place. There's a new, less materialistic tone to the list of things people care about. People are putting more emphasis on family and friends, on time to enjoy life rather than toys to enjoy life. People are moving away from, "My work is my life" to "My work is a job; my life is something more." This retreat from the excesses of the eighties may be sour grapes: "If I can't expect to move up in my career, I'll focus on other things." On the other hand, it may signal a recognition that when work is all there is in your life, having it all is not enough.

Columnist Ellen Goodman points out the absurdity of a materialistic orientation: "Normal is . . . getting dressed in clothes that you buy for work, driving through traffic in a car that you are still paying for, in order to get to the job that you need so you can pay for the clothes, car, and especially the house that you leave empty all day in order to afford to live in it."

Financial Consultants Joe Dominguez and Vicki Robin point out, "You're buying your money with your time." In their book, *Your Money or Your Life,* they emphasize frugality over a flashy lifestyle. Their book mirrors the dramatic shift in people's values. Today, many people say time is worth more than money. If the eighties was the era when we lived to work, the nineties is the decade when we work to live. Today, many people are deciding to trade status and salary for service and stability in such careers as social work and teaching. They're opting for a higher psychological paycheck.

Other people find that owning their own business tops any feelings of achievement they had with a job in corporate America. They like the idea that they are worth what they have to sell.

Other value shifts that impact how we think about work are under way.

Old Value	**New Value**
Sacrifice for the future	Self-fulfillment now
Higher standard of living	Quality of life
Society's definitions of success	Success on your own terms

Old Value	New Value
Faith in institutions	Faith in self
Outer-directed	Inner-directed

Examine your values. What do you believe about work? Are you making the transition from the old values to the new ones in the list above? It's not that the old is bad and the new is good. Just ask yourself what gives you satisfaction and a feeling of self-worth.

Believe in Yourself

Because it will deepen your understanding of yourself and bolster your ability to cope with whatever life brings, reading this book can increase your self-esteem. In chapters 6 through 10, we provide survival strategies, but your own self-esteem is the bedrock on which you must build your career security. Taking charge of your critic and turning that voice into a coach will help you support, not sabotage, your efforts as you implement the strategies. Refusing to hand over your entire life to your organization will allow you time and energy to take the steps you must to fireproof your career. Clarifying your values will help you determine your beliefs about work and its place in your life.

Chapter 4

The Language of Layoffs

In a "Peanuts" cartoon, Marcy whispers to Peppermint Patty: "I think the teacher is mad at you for not doing your homework. She says she may have to resort to castigation." Peppermint Patty replies, "They can't do something to you if you don't know what it means."

Peppermint Patty is wrong. They can do something to you if you don't know what it means. Language shapes perceptions, as every advertising copywriter and political "spin doctor" knows. And perceptions create language. We call it like we see it. Understanding the language of layoffs can help you understand society's attitude toward laid-off employees, and understanding the terminology of terminations can help you minimize its emotional impact on you.

Leah's friends were already sipping wine and chatting when she arrived at the restaurant for their monthly get-together. But the conversation stopped as she shucked her coat, yanked out a chair, plopped herself down and, having captured their attention, announced, "I was fired today." Her friends were shocked. Leah had received frequent promotions and raises and had brought many clients to the consulting firm she worked for. Her friends questioned her about the circumstances. She explained that, because of the recession, many people at the firm had been fired. Karen leaned toward her and said, forcefully, "Never say you have been fired. That means you weren't a good employee. Say, 'laid off.' "

That's true. The word *fired* now is usually reserved to describe the end of employment for a problem employee.

Even though her friends kept gently correcting her, Leah kept using the word *fired* as she talked about her situation. It was as if she couldn't think of any other word to use. That word best described her shock at being let go.

Words are powerful. Words create and reflect our perceptions. They evoke feelings. They carry along underlying meanings because of the way we've heard them used in the past or because of their origins. Sometimes, they deliberately manipulate or mask reality.

When we were kids, we chanted, "Sticks and stones can break my bones, but words can never hurt me." Remember what prompted us to sing out those words so bravely? Somebody had called us "fatty" or "four-eyes" or "fumble-fingers." And those words indeed had hurt. Unfortunately, most of the words dealing with losing a job are words that hurt. Even the phrase *losing a job* focuses on loss.

We've chosen to use the terms *laid off* and *layoff* in this book. Though they used to mean temporarily released from work, they now generally mean permanently released, often because of business conditions. They also are among the most neutral terms. There is one slang term that carries minimal negative connotations: Employees say they've been given a pink slip. The phrase refers to the practice some years ago of putting a pink slip notifying the employee of a layoff into his or her pay envelope. But the phrase is too unwieldy to use throughout a book like this and reminds people of temporary, blue-collar layoffs. As you'll discover in this chapter, other terms are much less neutral.

Victims of Violence

Some words cause us to think of those who are laid off as victims of a violent act. People are axed, booted, dropped, let go, bounced, bumped (as in bumped off?). They are given the chop or the old heave-ho. They are severed, eliminated, terminated—words with even more violent connotations.

At one time, IBM had a program called Management Initiated Attrition. Unfortunately, that meant the people affected were referred to as MIAs, letters that have traditionally stood for soldiers missing in action.

"At Tenneco," Alice explained, "we don't talk about people being laid off; we say, 'Joe got a package yesterday.'" The package is a collection of severance benefits. When we asked people what the word *package* reminded them of, they mentioned a letter bomb or a package that would detonate when opened—proof that even an innocuous word like *package* can have very negative connotations.

When employees are offered early retirement, some say, "I've been shot with the silver bullet," an oblique reference to their gray hair.

All these terms increase the laid-off employee's sense that he or she has been the victim of a violent—perhaps even fatal—attack.

"When they told me my job had been eliminated, it was as if they were saying I had been eliminated," says Keith. "I felt the dagger in my heart."

Worthless Discards

Some terms, like *corporate cast-offs,* imply that the laid-off employee has little value. People are canned, a word that has a variety of connotations, all negative: garbage can, waste can, toilet. Some companies call layoffs personnel surplus reductions and people are surplused, excessed, or made redundant. Slang terms that damage self-esteem include given the bum's rush, tossed out, sacked, and bagged. All of these terms may evoke feelings of worthlessness.

"How does it feel to be made redundant?" Regina says. "It feels like I'm a twin of a real, important human being and they only want one of us—the one who's real and important."

Outcasts

Some words make it clear that laid-off employees have been not only ejected, but also rejected and even shunned. The phrase *corporate cast-outs* is transformed into *outcasts.* People are shown the door or given the gate. People are handed their walking tickets, their walking papers, or, in more contemporary parlance, their running shoes. People are given the kiss-off, as in rejection by a loved one or the Mafia's kiss of death. Like baseball pitchers whose performance is causing their team to lose, people are sent to the showers. People are given the hook, a reference to the vaudeville practice of yanking performers offstage with a hook when the audience, bored with their performance, booed or threw rotten tomatoes.

"When I was shown the door, it was like I was being kicked out of my own home," says Roger. "I've never felt such a sense of rejection."

Roaches and Dust Bunnies

Other terms imply that the laid-off employees are less than human. Some companies call layoffs, *fumigations,* a term we usually associate with killing rodents or roaches. Other companies imply that employees are dirt or dust bunnies when they refer to layoffs as *cleaning house.* Still others say they are doing deadwood removal or hacking out the deadwood, pruning, or repotting (rootbound?) employees. Other woodsmen's terms are labor policies dubbed slash and burn or scorched earth. Some companies speak of executive culling, as if the executives were rotting fruit. To tie a can to an employee—another slang term for laying him off—calls to mind children tormenting stray dogs by tying cans to their tails. There's also a butcher shop vocabulary: Organizations trim the fat or cut to the bone to make the company lean and mean.

At one life insurance company, employee downsizing followed automation made possible by the installation of a new Cybertec computer. Employees picked up the word to explain that they had been laid off, saying, "I've been cyberteced."

"My boss called me into his office and proceeded to tell me that, unfortunately, the company was having to 'trim the fat,' " says Olivia. "I had a mental picture of the layer of fat I cut off a ham before I put it in the oven. But it was me he was talking about. I was that garbage."

Through Rose-Colored Glasses

In the last few years, consultants and human resource staffers have outdone themselves coining terms and phrases that sound impressive and institutional and, above all, impersonal.

These words are euphemistic—vaguely positive, neutral, or ambiguous terms used to talk about negative things. Euphemisms substitute a more pleasant, less objectionable way of saying something for a blunt or more direct way. We use euphemisms when reality is too threatening or upsetting. Rather than saying someone died, we say he passed away, went to his reward, or departed this life. These terms and others like them are a way of seeing things through linguistic rose-colored glasses, a way of smoothing off life's rough edges. Euphemisms make the unbearable bearable, the offensive inoffensive. Because they seek to soften it, they mask and manipulate reality.

Organizations have coined quite a list of impressive sounding words. Rather than saying straight out that they are laying people off, they imply they're merely adjusting the size of the workforce: *rightsizing, smartsizing, or downsizing.* (A companion term, *dumbsizing,* was coined to reflect the view that companies were not cutting fat, but muscle.) In the same spirit, organizations have conducted outplacements, force reductions, workforce adjustments, redeployments, vocational relocations, releases, negotiated departures, selective separations, and selective early retirements.

Some terms imply that the company is merely reshuffling job duties as they go about realigning, streamlining, rebundling, restructuring, or, as they said at National Semiconductor, "reshaping." Even more inventive creations include levels and layers analysis, career reassessments, skill mix adjustments, and workforce imbalance corrections.

Other words do imply a reduction in staff: *destaffing, dehiring, degrowing, delayering, derecruiting, redundancy eliminations, proactive downsizing, coerced transitions, downleveling,* and the mysterious *creepback.* Bank of America has released resources. The U.S. Navy is engaging in drawdowns.

Sometimes, layoffs are positioned as moves to enhance productivity, as companies implement chemistry changes, operations improvement programs, work reengineering, employee repositioning, operation excellence efforts, and efficiencies.

Some terms defy translation. Digital instituted "involuntary methodologies."

All these euphemistic words are designed to appeal to boards of directors and stockholders. They take the focus off people and put it on the organization chart and the bottom line. Even Wal-Mart, one of the most successful companies of the nineties, has had something they call "a normal payroll adjustment" now and then.

Notice that most of these phrases use long, Latin-based words and that the terms often are very formal. Notice, too, the avoidance of any reference to the people involved, except as the workforce, a term that lumps individuals into a faceless mass. The terms also overlook the skills and capabilities of individuals, as if they don't matter.

For the individual, these organizational activities translate into disemployment, job elimination, indefinite idling, or involuntary separation. Employees are riffed (an acronym for *reduction in force*), furloughed, dismissed, deselected, and transitioned.

A layoff by any other name is still a layoff to the people involved, and the hurtful language does have an impact on how employees feel about the experience.

Survivors

Most insidious of all the words in the language of layoffs is the term *survivor.* Survivors are people who have **not** been laid off. By extension, that makes people who **have** been laid off nonsurvivors. Imagine what it does, psychologically, to a laid-off employee to be among those who have not survived. If your organization has had layoffs and you have survived, you are encouraged to think of your job as life itself. The term relates in our minds to Darwin's phrase, "survival of the fittest."

Psychologists who worked with survivors of Nazi concentration camps have identified what they call survivor's guilt. Corporate survivors suffer a version of that malaise. "Why did George get the ax and not me?" they wonder. They feel guilty because they may not be able to come up with a satisfactory answer to that question. Because they feel guilty, they shun the laid-off employee—someone who may have been a good friend in the past—just at the time that person needs their support the most. Survivors sense that they are betraying their friends and feel even more guilt. And so, "survivors" often distance themselves from the person who has been laid off, as if that person has a communicable disease.

Workers are hesitant to express sympathy to their laid-off colleagues. If they do say something sympathetic, won't that imply that their all-knowing organization may have made a mistake? Unthinkable! Surviving employees must maintain their belief in the fairness and even-handedness of their employers.

Survivors go through elaborate machinations to protect their sense of security. "Surely," they think, "there must have been a good reason for Joe to have been laid off. He must have done something wrong." We often blame victims for their misfortunes, even when there was no way the victims could have prevented them. Rape victims, for example, sometimes are blamed for the attack, as when someone says, "She was asking for it. She shouldn't have worn that miniskirt." If we can convince ourselves that the victim failed to take appropriate precautions, then we reason that all we need to do to avoid a similar disaster is to take those precautions.

If, as the rumors about layoffs have circulated through the grapevine, the atmosphere at work has been awful (as it inevitably is) and if morale plummets (as it inevitably does) as the rumored layoffs actually take place, the survivors may actually feel jealous or envious of those who have been laid off. They, too, want out of there. Henry said, "I'm not quite sure who the lucky ones are. Us (the survivors) or them (the laid-off employees)." Some survivors, however, can't risk expressing those feelings, even to themselves.

The survivors may sense that they'll have to work even harder in the lean and mean organization to cope with the workload of those who have been laid off. As the organization dumps sometimes unfamiliar and often less prestigious tasks on survivors, they resent the extra work. The survivors are angry, but afraid to express that anger toward the organization. They may displace it and aim their anger toward those who have been laid off. That's irrational, to be sure, but it's safer.

Minimize the Impact

While you're still employed, you can make a conscious decision not to use the word *survivor* when you talk about yourself or others. If you continue to use that word, you set yourself up to think of yourself as a nonsurvivor should you ever be laid off. You must believe that, even if your current job goes away, you will survive. Your job is not your life. Substitute more neutral words, such as *stayers* and *leavers* or *maintainers* and *movers.* Encourage your organization to use terms that reflect reality and are less emotionally loaded.

Of course, it isn't the words themselves that hurt; it's the feelings that the words evoke and the actuality of being laid off that wound us. You can't do much about the language of layoffs, but by understanding it, you can reduce its emotional impact on you.

Know that you are not your job title nor your company affiliation. Seek your self-esteem in your own character and competence. These are assets that you control. No organization can take them away from you.

Chapter 5

The Anatomy of Loss

As you understand the ramifications of job loss, your anxiety will diminish and your determination to take charge of your own career will increase. First, you need to understand how people are laid off, so that your expectations are in line with reality. Next, you will be able to fireproof your feelings by getting acquainted with the predictable emotional responses to losing a job. Your reactions to job loss begin even before you are notified that you are being let go. The loss cycle covers the entire time from the day you first hear whispered rumors about layoffs to the day you can look back without bitterness. Understanding what usually happens emotionally to people who are laid off will help you move more quickly toward creating your new life. Finally, you will learn how to help others in your life deal with the possibility of your being laid off.

How People Are Laid Off

Companies may or may not have well-thought-out plans about how people will be let go. Execution (pardon the pun) is often less than ideal.

Do not expect that your notification will be done in a humane and professional manner. If you are treated well, you're an exception. Your organization may have talked about being a family in the past. You don't expect your family to dispose of you unceremoniously. The stronger your expectations of being treated a certain way, the stronger your anger when things don't happen as you had thought they would. Expect the worst. That way, you may be pleasantly surprised. At the very least, you'll take it less personally and won't waste your energy on being angry at the methods used to lay you off.

Consider these scenarios.

- Mary, a human resources specialist with a department store, had just finished laying off 300 workers when her boss called her into his office. "Sorry, Mary," he said. "Now that you're finished, you're not in our budget."
- The executives—a few hundred of them—of a manufacturing plant were invited to a meeting in a hotel ballroom. A tape-recorded announcement was used to dismiss them, one and all, on the spot.
- Employees of an Oklahoma company have computer terminals at home. Every morning, first thing, they run to their computers. If they can log on, they still have a job, if not, they are laid off.
- Reggie found out he'd been laid off when, arriving at work, he put his card key into the slot to open the door to the building, and the key didn't work. His code had been deactivated.
- A stockbroker's first hint that he was out of work was a certified letter that he received one Saturday morning, informing him that his employer was dropping his insurance coverage.
- Gladys, in the finance department, was entering data on her computer when a security person showed up, removed her hands from the keyboard, told her to pick up her purse, and escorted her out of the building.
- Roy had been working long hours and had not taken a single day of vacation during the entire year. Finally, he decided

to take his kids to Worlds of Fun, a theme park, for the day. Conscientious employee that he was, he called his office around noon, just to check in. His secretary told him he'd been laid off.

- Caroline called her office from the airport before boarding a flight that would take her to a management meeting she was scheduled to attend in Atlanta. ''Oh, there's no need for you to go,'' she was told. ''You've been laid off.''
- Larry pulled into the company's parking garage and headed to his reserved parking place, but there was another car parked there and—he got out of his car to check—another name on the slot.
- Employees at one company were invited to one of two meetings, held simultaneously. In one meeting, attendees were told they were ''winners;'' in the other, attendees were told they were ''losers'' and were laid off.
- April was on her honeymoon when she got a call from the office informing her that she'd been laid off.
- Heather's boss invited her to breakfast at the Mansion on Turtle Creek in Dallas and fired her over the omelets. Later, the boss told Heather, ''I decided to tell you at the restaurant because I didn't want you to get angry and scream at me.'' The ploy didn't work. Heather created quite a scene in the upscale restaurant.
- ''The letter terminating my employment was terse,'' says Wes. ''There was no mention of my contributions to the company. It was signed by someone whose name I didn't recognize.''

The Case of the Shrunken Org Chart

''Picture this,'' Julie says. ''For several months, rumors of layoffs have been whispered by everyone in the company, from top management to the mail room clerk. Everyone is uneasy and upset. If it happens, this would be the fourth time in three years this particular company has cut staff.

"The Top Dog calls an all-staff meeting for 11 A.M. on a Friday. When we're all assembled, he distributes a memo outlining a mechanism by which all salaries will be cut. Even though no one is happy about the cut, you can hear people breathing a sigh of relief. At least, we think, no one will be laid off.

"At the end of much discussion about the pay cuts, another memo is distributed. This one is a staff structure chart. The boss says, 'Now, if you don't see your job on here, that means . . . ' And so he cut staff, including one employee who had more than thirty years of service with the company and who was five months from her already-determined retirement date. No joke. I was there."

The Case of the Bizarre Broadcast

"I was in my office," Pam said, "when I overheard, through the supposedly soundproof glass of the production studio next door, a promotional announcement going out to the listening audience. The promo was for a new afternoon show, starting that day, and named two other people as the hosts."

After that happened to her, Pam began to collect other bizarre stories about how people were let go.

One involved a boss who kept a Polaroid camera in his desk. After the selected employee came into his office, he'd snap that person's picture, hand it to him, and say, 'I thought you'd like to have a snapshot of yourself on your last day.'

Another good one involved the boss who was a Civil War buff. He had a small army of toy soldiers on his desk. He'd call in his victim, point to one of the figures, and say, 'This is you.' Then he'd flip it into oblivion with his finger.

The Case of the Disappearing Responsibilities

"The executive told me my job would be 'duplicative,' after the consolidation of two similar departments," remembers Sue, who was given six months to find a new job within the company. "He explained that my skills were 'more transportable' than my counterpart's, and so I was being asked to 'relocate' myself inside the company. I felt like a commodity rather than a human being, like extra baggage. I was wary of showing loyalty and did not trust anybody at the company. I became depressed and relatively dysfunctional at home, while putting on a good act at the office. I felt like I had been caught in an undertow and was being slowly drowned. Dog-paddling was the only way I could stay afloat. I had forgotten how to swim. My belief in myself was draining away. Lifeguards were nowhere to be seen. I had to beg for support from Human Resources.

"Soon, I had no responsibilities, nothing for which I was accountable. I watched my job being sliced apart and apportioned to the remaining staff while I literally bled inside.

"At that point, I panicked and jumped to the first open position in the company, one with lower status in which my skills and abilities are not being used. Yes, I'm working, but my attitude toward this company will never be the same."

What You Lose When You Lose a Job

Unemployment statistics and newspaper headlines about layoffs can't begin to convey what it feels like to lose a job, to get out of bed in the morning with no place to go and nothing to do, cut off from everything that is familiar.

We've asked people in our workshops to list what they would lose if they lost their jobs. Here's what they say:

- My paycheck
- The ability to go to the bank and borrow money
- My life, medical, dental, and disability insurance
- My profit-sharing plan
- My savings plan (not the savings in the plan, but the ability to contribute to the plan regularly)
- My stock plan (the ability to continue to buy stock through the company)
- Tax benefits: my 401(k) plan, pretax reimbursement accounts for medical care that's not covered by my insurance, reimbursement for child care or for care for an elderly family member
- Perks: half-price tickets to cultural and sporting events, club memberships, access to a health club, and free parking
- The neighborhood where my office is located: stores where I habitually shop, restaurants I'm used to, my dry cleaners
- Self-esteem, self-confidence, a feeling of self-worth
- Training opportunities
- Educational assistance benefits (I'm in the middle of my master's degree)
- Friends, contacts, the companionship and teamwork of the office
- My office (I love the furniture, the view, seeing the trees outside my window bloom in the spring and turn red in the fall.)
- A place where I have all my books, my diplomas, my awards; a place where I am organized
- Routine, structure (My daily schedule.)
- Identity and identification with an organization—how I introduce myself, the feeling of being a part of a company everyone in town knows and respects
- My status in my family, among my friends and acquaintances, in my profession
- My place in society
- Membership in the middle class
- My support system—everything from my secretary to the company's travel agent to the photocopy machine

- A sense of accomplishment, purpose, and contribution
- The work itself—I love my work

You lose a lot when you lose a job.

"I had a jacket with the company logo on it," remembers Alvin. "After I was laid, off, I burned it. I had loved wearing that jacket when a bunch of the guys would get together and play baseball. It was agony to stand there and watch it burn."

What would you lose? Make a list of the things that you would miss if your job disappeared today. Rank the items on your list. Which are most important to you? Is there any way you could cover these possible losses or reduce the impact of the loss of these things on you? How?

As you think through which aspects of your worklife you would miss most, use the five strategies outlined in chapters 6 through 10 to develop substitutes, alternatives, new support systems, and expanded lifestyle choices. For example, if you discover that most of your friends and contacts are people you know at work, then focus on networking to build stronger relationships with people outside your office.

The Loss Cycle

Because it's so traumatic, job loss is the third most severe loss people can suffer. In many ways, people's reactions to losing their jobs duplicate their reactions to the number one loss, death of a loved one, and the number two loss, divorce.

Researchers say that it's difficult to predict exactly how a particular individual will react to being laid off, but that many people report going through a sequence of emotional stages. Some people move quickly through the various stages after they have been laid off; others move slowly, taking as much as a year or more to complete the cycle; others move forward and then drop back to repeat a stage in a sort of two steps forward, one step back pattern.

Throughout the loss cycle, people report feeling a lack of control, increased stress, mounting anxiety, and moments of heart-stopping fear. As you understand how people typically react to job loss, you will be able to explain your feelings to yourself. You'll know that you aren't going crazy when these emotions occur. You'll be able to explain the cycle to your spouse or partner, so that he or she understands your emotional roller-coaster and can provide appropriate support.

Worry and Concern

Rumors about the possibility of layoffs surface. Rumors almost always precede any official statement from the organization. People may work longer, if not harder, as they try to make sure they will not be laid off. But, overall, productivity declines as people spend a lot of time and energy speculating about what will happen.

Resignation

As time goes on, one way people cope is by giving up. They say, "What will be, will be." This passivity reflects people's acceptance that layoffs are something they can't control. There's a feeling that "What I do doesn't really matter. It's out of my hands."

Jockeying for Position

If people believe that the layoff will be selective, that some people in their department or area will be spared, they may aggressively try to position themselves as star performers. Backstabbing and political infighting escalate as people jockey for favorite son or daughter status with the boss. Cooperation and teamwork disappear as employees are pitted against each other.

If you are nervous about your job security with your current employer, you may already be on the roller-coaster of emotions that accompanies impending job loss. You may already be feeling the emotions associated with one of the first three stages of the loss cycle.

Notification of Layoff

People are notified that they have been or will be laid off. The most immediate feeling may be a sense of relief that the waiting is over. That relief is usually short-lived, but some people report that the uncertainty of not knowing whether they would be laid off was more stressful than the reality. People say, "Once the ambiguity was gone, and it was clear that my future would take place someplace else, I felt better."

Shock

In this stage, occurring immediately after they are told they will be laid off, people often are numb and unresponsive. They find it difficult to do anything, even to talk.

Denial

In this stage, a common reaction is, "I can't believe this is really happening to me." In one study, 80 percent of laid-off employees said they were surprised. That's the "I can't believe this" reaction. Some people, after they have been notified, race around trying to finish a project or a report as if they refuse to believe that their job has ended. They imagine a letter being delivered or the phone ringing and someone giving them the message, "It was all a mistake. Of course, we aren't going to lay you off." Or, they imagine that they are immediately hired by another department or unit of the company, that someone or something will save them. They can't imagine how the organization will survive without them, without their special knowledge and expertise.

Sometimes people say, with the clarity of 20/20 hindsight, "I knew it. I knew it was going to happen." They gain a small sense of control by saying, "I predicted it. I'm not surprised."

Anger

In this stage, people become angry. They say things like, "They can't do this to me. I'll show them. I don't deserve this. Where's my lawyer?" They ventilate a lot. They talk about how loyal they were and how the organization betrayed them. The greater the personal and emotional investment they had in their jobs and the more they trusted that the company would take care of them, the angrier they are at having the rug pulled out from under them.

Ironically, the people who are let go often are those with the longest tenure, those who feel they have been the most loyal. More people over fifty-five are out of work than ever before. They may feel that they have been discriminated against because of their age. In reality, their age may be less a determining factor than the fact that, in the company's eyes, they are overqualified and overpaid.

Typically, men exhibit more anger than women do. They sometimes deny their feelings of depression, guilt, and grief. Women, on the other hand, deny and internalize their anger, turning it instead into depression, guilt, and grief. People who get in touch with all these feelings move more quickly through the cycle.

Bargaining

In this stage, people fantasize about steps they could have taken in the past to avoid being laid off. Round and round they go in their minds, like a hamster running a wheel. They rehash and replay past events and conversations. They mentally revise what they did or should have done over the past months. They rewrite history in their minds.

They also fantasize about steps they still could take to avoid being laid off, even though they've already been given their notice. They may think, "I'd do anything to get my job back. Why didn't they give me more warning? If they'd give me another chance, things would be different." They imagine negotiating with the boss and being able to reverse the situation to get themselves rehired.

Guilt

In this stage, people ask, "Why me?" They conclude, "I must have done something to deserve this." They blame themselves. They are ashamed. They revisit in their minds every lapse or failure or rejection in their lives. The disappointments and hurts of a lifetime come rushing back into their minds.

Depression

In this stage, people think, "I'm no good. It's no wonder they don't want me." They gain or lose weight, sleep too much or too little. They are embarrassed and humiliated by what they believe is a personal failure. They hide away and hit bottom.

Grief

In this stage, people reflect on what they have lost. They are painfully aware of all of the consequences of losing their job. They are sad. They mourn. They cry. "It's the death of a life you loved," says one social worker. Even if they didn't love their jobs, they mourn the death of the familiar.

Acceptance

In this stage, people begin to have a sense of getting on with it. Their broken hearts are mending. They are ready to let go of the past. They say, "There's nothing I can do about it." They feel tiny twinges of excitement about the future. They say things like, "Today is the first day of the rest of my life." They begin to reexamine what they want to do with their lives and what changes they can or should make. They refocus. They create a vision of what life can and will be like for them.

Involvement and Commitment

In this stage, people are ready to become involved with a new organization and to make a commitment to that organization, although it is often a different kind of work commitment than they have ever made in the past. They recognize that the greater your investment in your job, the more devastating it is to lose. They vow in the future to maintain a better balance between work and the rest of their lives.

Recognition of Ability

After people have gone through the crisis of job loss and regained employment, they often believe that they are stronger for the experience. They believe that the layoff was a good thing to have gone through, even if it wasn't a good thing to be going through. They relish their proven ability to get by, to weather the storm, to show their character, and to take it on the chin and get up fighting. They value the experience gained and their increased self-awareness. They say that they have much less fear about the future and about their economic security. In short, they often feel that they have learned valuable lessons about how to cope with the uncertain future.

If you know how people typically react to job loss, you can move more quickly through the stages that make it difficult to begin again. You may not be ready for a new job until you have dealt with the unresolved conflicts and experienced all the emotional swings of job loss. To move through the stages quickly if you are laid off, consider the following suggestions.

- Make sure you understand the process. Review the loss cycle.
- Keep a journal. A private log of your thoughts and feelings can help you get in touch with and sort through your emotions. Research indicates that people who keep journals, not only move through the stages more quickly, but also find reemployment more quickly.
- Ask for strong support from family, friends, and especially from other people who have been through the experience.

Positive Results

There's evidence that middle-aged workers who cling to job security and, out of fear, hang on to jobs they hate are more likely to experience professional and personal burnout. These folks are far worse off than their colleagues who change careers, even if that change is involuntary. It sounds trite, but, for many people, being laid off is a blessing in disguise. People who reassess their goals, their values, and their strengths and then move on have a much greater sense of psychological and personal well-being than people who stagnate in situations they dislike just for that paycheck. The ability to make effective transitions is one key to living a rich and fulfilling life. Fireproofing yourself is the process of preparing for career transitions.

Excessive Reactions

Occasionally, people who have been laid off react with violence. Homicide in the workplace is the fastest-growing form of murder. Researchers estimate that there is a 200 to 300 percent increase in murder by people who have been let go and blame their supervisors or manager or the person who gave them the bad news. Tom Harpley of National Trauma Services in San Diego was interviewed for an article in the *Personnel Journal.* He says people who commit murder in the workplace see work as the source of their identity. Because their interpersonal relationships are shallow, a layoff means more than the loss of income. It's equated with actual loss of existence. "When terminated, the person feels he has lost his life. . . . So [he thinks], why not take a few people with him?" Harpley compares the laid-off employee's need for revenge to the reaction of a person who has lost a loved one to murder: The desire to see the perpetrator pay for the crime, perhaps even die, becomes paramount, even though such an action can never bring back the victim.

Such violence, then, is not irrational or random; it is a logical consequence of an excessive reaction to job loss.

Other reactions, though they may not be life-threatening, are debilitating. Some people become aggressive. Some people resort to spouse and child abuse. Some people abuse alcohol or drugs. Some people become suicidal. Many people suffer physical reactions, such as cardiovascular problems, high blood pressure, headaches, or stomachaches.

Research suggests that adverse affects are most extreme among people who do not have a strong network of friends and relatives and who have had the strongest attachment to their jobs. These people typically made the workplace the source of all their self-esteem and friendships, as well as their incomes. And, the more people blame themselves rather than something impersonal, like the economy, for example, the more severe their negative reactions.

Dealing with Significant Others

Ideally, your loved ones will support and encourage you if you lose your job. Often, however, your job loss is as traumatic or even more so for your partner or family as it is for you. The most important people in your life may be unable to provide the support you need. Divorce increases among laid-off workers. Some spouses become resentful, blaming, rejecting, and openly hostile. Children may cling, need more attention, or regress to babyish behaviors such as thumb-sucking or bed-wetting. They may be angry and frightened. They need to express their feelings and be reassured that they will be taken care of, just at the moment their parents may feel least able to provide that reassurance.

Stories abound of laid-off male executives who keep the layoff a secret from their wives for weeks or even months. It's very important to talk over the possibility of being laid off now, before the situation actually occurs, and determine what special challenges you will need to deal with in your relationship. Every relationship has a balance of power based on status and money. That power structure will shift if one of you is laid off. Educate your spouse about the loss cycle. If your partner is able to accept your feelings as you work your way through the inevitable emotional ups and downs, it will be easier for you to deal with the move beyond those feelings of loss. Understanding the cycle will help your partner listen creatively to what you say. Your partner will be able to help you determine which stage you're going through.

Enlist your partner's participation as you create your career security plan. Encourage your partner to read this book. Work together to prepare yourselves so that, together, you can achieve long-term career security.

Part II

Survival Strategies

Chapter 6

Liberate Your Mind

You probably haven't received a memo about this. Nobody's called a meeting to announce it. It hasn't been discussed in the company newsletter. However, we bet you've noticed that something's going on. There's been a change in the underlying, but unwritten, contract between employer and employee, a change in the unofficial agreements that define your relationship with your employer, a change in the bond between you and the organization. This change demands that you liberate your mind from old ways of thinking if you want to thrive in the workplace of tomorrow.

Evidence from the Edge

Trend spotting may simply be a matter of noticing a statistic that seems to reveal a major social change, such as noticing when people working in the service sector begin to outnumber people working in the manufacturing sector. However, when we look for indicators of the change in expectations between employer and employee, there are few statistics.

Instead, there are comments, like the advice Jack Welch, head of General Electric, gave to his employees: "Face reality as it is, not as it was or as you wish it were.''

There are predictions, like this one from Robert Reich, Secretary of Labor: ''Companies will move their factories to a lower wage place, they'll lay off or fire their workers, they'll substitute automated equipment for their employees. They'll do whatever is necessary to improve the bottom line.''

There are actions, like organizations notifying employees that they must take a more active role in accumulating and managing their own savings for retirement and must pay a larger portion of the costs of their medical benefits.

There's the 1990 Conference Board survey that revealed a new, hard-nosed, hands-off attitude on the part of employers. In a nutshell, those companies surveyed said, ''Don't rely on us to manage your career. You must be self-sufficient. You must decide for yourself whether you should stay with the firm or go elsewhere to further your career goals.''

These hints may be all the announcement you'll get that corporate paternalism is a thing of the past. As employees of the phone company, used to thinking of the corporation as maternal, put it, ''Ma Bell is dead.'' The old contract, one that seemed to promise lifetime job security in return for loyalty and dedication beyond the call of duty, is null and void. Short-term profit pressures exacerbated by long-term, worldwide economic shifts have destroyed it.

As difficult as it is to admit, the truth is that no matter how hard you work or how loyal and dedicated you are, your job is no longer secure.

What the new agreements between employer and employee will be like is still unclear. The rules of the game are being invented while we play the game. One general manager of human resources planning at a Fortune 500 company admitted his confusion. ''We're working to figure out what will be in the 'new' contract. It's evolving; we're not yet sure ourselves what is going to happen,'' he said.

How do these changes affect you?

It's time for you to take over responsibility for your career. It's time to put managing your career on your own agenda, where it belongs. It's time to stop waiting for ''them'' to do something. It's time to stop griping about why "they" don't hand out promotions like they used to. It's time to stop moaning about the way "they" go about eliminating jobs.

It's not easy to adopt this new mind-set. To take charge, you must give up some cherished ideas about your relationship with the company you work for. You must examine—and reject—some old patterns of thinking and behaving. You must deliberately set out to develop a new relationship with your employer, a new bond with your organization. Oh, how we long to be taken care of! Even in the best of circumstances, though, relying on an institution to provide something as vital as your career security is risky. Ultimately, you must take care of yourself.

The Old Contract

The old contract was based on two unstated yet powerful ideas.

- Your job security is guaranteed by your employer.
- Father knows best.

Your Job Is Safe

Once upon a time, you could bank on job security. If you worked hard and were loyal, you could count on being rewarded for your efforts and could settle into the security of lifetime employment. "The understanding was ingrained in our culture: If you do a good job, you'll be taken care of," said a top executive at Control Data Corporation. You were expected to demonstrate your loyalty by working long hours or by relocating your family if your boss said, "We need you in Cleveland." The implied promise was, "If you follow, your future will be assured."

Since the mid-eighties, it's been hard to pick up a newspaper or watch the evening news without hearing about every conceivable kind and size of organization going through every conceivable kind of change on the way to becoming radically different and noticeably leaner. Some of the largest companies have dismissed half of their workers. With the military "drawing down" and government "reinventing" itself, no sector of the economy is safe.

Some companies seemed to want to hang on to the idea of job security as badly as the employees. In efforts to avoid layoffs, these employers tried cutting costs by eliminating overtime. They brought back inside the work that had been subcontracted to outside vendors. They let temporary employees go first. They trained employees at all levels to look for waste and find "best cost" solutions. They encouraged attrition, sometimes offering outrageously generous financial packages to people who were willing to retire early. Finally, there was no place else to turn. Layoffs were inevitable.

A majority of companies did not, and are not, going to these lengths to avoid layoffs. They started slashing their workforces at the first sign of pressure for higher quarterly profits and have continued to cut even as they achieved or regained profitability. Some are laying off people, even though profitability today is not an issue. They're concerned about positioning themselves for the more intense competition that they believe is just around the corner. The inviolate idea of job security has been violated.

Father Knows Best

In some companies, not too many years ago, even some very personal decisions became company matters, and nobody blinked an eye. The company was like an extended family; the president was a strict father, who in making employees toe the line, had his "children's" welfare at heart. Cleyson L. Brown, founder of the local telephone company group that is now part of Sprint, disseminated his fatherly advice in the form of a jingle, printed in the company magazine in 1918.

"Eat less, drink less, and smoke less, and wear your clothes
a little longer.
Make it a principle. Make it a religion. Make it a habit.
There is not a human being in the United States that cannot

> exist on nine-tenths of what he does exist on. Save the other tenth.''

When such exhortations didn't have the desired effect, Brown issued the following edict, making such saving mandatory. ''Every employee of the United Telephone Company and Associated Companies will be required to save ten percent of his income, starting on July 1st (1922) or seek affiliation with another company.'' Brown justified his policy this way: ''Advice was tried and it failed. So after careful consideration and investigation, I determined that if the employee would not save voluntarily, it was perfectly justifiable, for his own good, to make him save.''

We may mourn the end of paternalism, the end of being taken care of at work, but in some ways, the good old days weren't that great. Today's employees can't imagine a company insisting on monitoring how they spend or save their money.

Workers in companies that still operate on paternalistic philosophies may not realize how much control they have given over to their employers. In a paternalistic company, employees spend a great deal of energy deferring to authority. If you work for a company like this, you feel it necessary to ''read'' the people above you and to spend long hours figuring out what they want you to do. You feel you should blend in, be compliant, and wait to act until those above you give the order. You know it's wise to hold back, spout the party line, hide your feelings, and kowtow to the top. Without even being told, you know that the way to get ahead is to surrender your independence in return for belonging. But, as you seek approval, ask permission, become increasingly careful, and put a lid on expressing yourself, you become more and more dependent. Then you rationalize your dependency by thinking of it as a bargain: ''Because I have given the organization control over my work life, they owe me one. I deserve safety and security in return.''

The deal, as it has developed over the years, includes letting the organization send you on your way along a predetermined career path, dictating to you when to learn a new skill, notifying you when you are to be mysteriously or inevitably promoted, deciding what to include in your benefits package, and determining how your retirement will be funded.

What About You?

In one of Gary Larson's delightful "The Far Side" cartoons, the settlers have circled their wagons to fend off an attack by the Indians. The Indians are shooting not regular arrows but flaming arrows. One settler can't believe his eyes and says to the guy next to him, "Are they allowed to *do* that?" Most of us experience the same kind of amazement as we watch employers break the old bargains.

Max DePree, author of *Leadership Jazz,* says, "Believe it or not, one of a leader's chief concerns is the problem of betrayal. Many kinds of betrayals take place in organizations. . . . Most betrayals come to light after the fact, after one party silently abandons a goal or a commitment."

Most companies have silently abandoned their commitment to guarantee job security and to guide your career.

Notice the unwritten assumptions or bargains you think you have with your employer. One way to gauge the extent to which you still buy into the old contract is to become aware of the amount of betrayal you feel when you imagine your boss saying to you, "I'm sorry. We have to lay you off."

Another way to uncover the psychological contract you believe you have with your employer is to complete these sentences:

"If I'm loyal, then . . ."
"If I work more than forty hours a week, then . . ."
"If I keep my nose clean, then . . ."
"If I make my boss happy, then . . ."
"If I'm the only person who really knows how to do this job, then . . ."
"If I remind people how long I've been here, then . . ."
"If I'm agreeable, then . . ."

Did you finish any of these "If . . . then . . ." bargains by expressing expectations of safety and security? It's not that wanting security is bad, it's just that the way to ensure your career safety has changed. The word *dependent* literally means *hanging*—not a very secure position. Contrast that image with "standing on your own two feet"—a grounded and secure position. Who would choose to dangle?

We do, though. People assume a dependant relationship with their work organizations for two reasons: We have learned to be dependent, and organizations in the past have expected and supported that dependency.

In our first relationships, as children within our families, we are dependent by necessity. Human biology dictates a long period of dependency. In the twentieth century, children may be dependent financially—and therefore somewhat dependent emotionally—until they are finished with college or even graduate school. In the current economy, young adults, even married couples, have returned to the nest because they can't earn enough to live on their own.

Schools also teach dependency. Even in the most student-centered classroom, the teacher still is the court of last resort, the primary source of information, the final authority. The teacher is in control and has the ultimate responsibility.

Military service also provides training in following orders and sacrificing individuality for the common good. The military still refers to children and spouses as "dependents," to the annoyance of many self-sufficient mates. Old ways of thinking persist.

By the time we reach the workforce, we have learned our lessons well. We know how to deal with the unequal distribution of power that characterizes the employer/employee relationship, just as it characterized the parent/child, teacher/student, and leader/follower relationships.

Remember that wonderful movie, *The Wizard of Oz?* When Dorothy finally is granted an audience with the supposedly all-powerful Wizard, the hides behind a screen and thunders out amid clouds of smoke, "I am Oz, the great and terrible." Dorothy, quaking in her red shoes, those shoes that give her power she doesn't yet know she has, replies, "I am Dorothy, the small and meek." When it comes to corporate life, most people are Dorothys.

The other reason that the dependency model prevails is that organizations are set up to encourage it. Work is segmented into tasks done by various departments. The hierarchy of the pyramid forces responsibility to the top, as employees check with managers, who run things up the flagpole and launch trial balloons so as not to surprise vice presidents, who bounce difficult decisions up to the executive committee, which delivers unanswered questions to the CEO, who waits for the board of directors to set policy.

Control is valued more than creativity. Rules and regulations, policies, and procedures dominate the culture. Conformance is valued more than contribution. Group norms depress individual initiative.

Almost all organizations have realized that they must break away from this old model and many management initiatives are focusing on changing the way things get done. Yet, few organizations can say that they have been successful in eliminating the insidious dependency that has been a tradition and that has molded the structure of companies and the behavior within that structure.

How dependent are you in the relationship you have with your organization?

When we asked our workshop participants to describe the unwritten agreements that characterize the old contract, they came up with these ideas. Put a check mark next to any that are, or were, true for you and add any other ideas that come to mind.

- I have guaranteed stability.
- I have the safety of belonging to something permanent.
- My upward mobility is almost a given.
- My rewards will be tied to loyalty as well as to performance.
- There will be no layoffs—ever!
- The organization is tradition-driven.
- The company is responsible for my career development.

- The important decisions are made by the big guys behind the scenes. My role is just to carry out those decisions and not to question them.
- My career is in the hands of others.
- I give my soul for my salary.
- There's a clear shot at the upward ladder.
- I spout the company line; no back talk.
- Between departments, there are boundaries that you dare not cross without permission.
- There's a stable organizational chart.
- There are good benefits.
- My retirement is secure.
- I know where I fit in; I know when to stand up and sit down.
- I defer to higher-ups even when I think—or know—they're wrong.
- I try to make all news good news when talking to those above me.
- The company is organized around fixed job descriptions and departments. Everybody knows his place.
- There is little mixing with people more than one or two rungs above or below me in the hierarchy.
- I work hard and do what I'm told to do.
- I put my work ahead of my family and personal interests.
- The rules are clear.
- I know to always be faithful and obedient.
- I'm told only what they decide I need to know.

How closely does this description fit your experience? As you can see, some of the phrases depicting life under the old contract sound nostalgic, as in "I have the safety of belonging to something permanent." Some sound angry, as in "I give my soul for my salary." Some reflect the cocooned safety of belonging but don't leave much room for autonomy, such as in "I know where I fit in." And some are purely descriptive. In some ways the contract sounds like the parent/child relationship, as in "Be faithful and obedient" and "I'm told only what they decide I need to know."

Jerome M. Rostow, president of the Work in America Institute, has characterized the massive downsizings of the past few years as, "the ripping apart of the social contract." Consider the group that has been most distressed by the tearing up of the old contract—the men who have been loyal to one company for decades. One thirty-three-year veteran manager who was forced to take early retirement at age fifty-seven said, "I knew in the back of my mind several years ago that things had leveled off for me and I should get out, but I kept believing, hoping the company would take care of me. How can they do this to me after I've given them all these years?"

Younger employees have also bought into the promise of security. They believe just as much in the old contract, but they don't feel quite as betrayed, perhaps because they have invested less. Overall, we give up too much and the price of belonging is too high.

Think about these questions. Your answers will give you a good indication of how dependent you are on your current organization.

- Do you delight in introducing yourself as an employee of your company? The amount of pleasure you take in announcing your affiliation with your organization is an indication of the degree to which you rely on that organization for your identity, self-esteem, and self-worth.
- How careful are you as you communicate with people above you in the hierarchy? Do you rarely tell the whole truth? Do you doctor messages or soften them before relaying them to those in power? Are you wary of expressing the truth as you see it?
- How comfortable are you bringing a problem to the attention of the higher-ups? In many organizations, employees warn each other, "If you stand up, you will be shot." One organization set up employee meetings and encouraged workers to ask questions. When one man stood up and asked a question, the CEO ridiculed him and told him if he didn't know the answer to *that* question, he had no business working there. There were no more questions. Employees learn quickly.

- How much do you modify your natural behavior? Do you watch those with more power to pick up on the slightest clues that tip you as to the correct or preferred way to act? In a training course at work, Sean took a quiz that, among other things, compared his natural behavior to his work behavior. He noticed that he had made quite an adaptation to fit in. After he had been in business for himself for several years, he took the quiz again. This time, his natural style and work style matched exactly. What kind of accommodation have you made to become one of the gang at work?
- How eager are you for a pat on the back? Does it mean more to you when the boss gives you an "Attaboy" than when you know, deep down, that you have done an excellent job? Kenna worked for thirteen years for a boss whose idea of feedback was, "I'll tell you if I'm unhappy." She said she could count on the fingers of one hand the times he'd said "Good job" to her. She spent a lot of time hungering for his approval.
- How consistently do you check before you act? Different corporate cultures call this behavior by different names: running things up the flagpole, preselling ideas, floating trial balloons.
- How often do you complain that "they" won't let you do something—without ever checking it out? Employees create elaborate rules and restrictions based on what they think "they" want. These assumptions are often based on old stories rather than current realities. Complaining about the anonymous "they" provides an easy out, acts as an excuse for playing it safe, and gives people a reason to avoid taking risks.

Once you have become aware of the old contract and how it has affected you, you're ready to consider adopting a new set of assumptions and agreements that will outline a new relationship with your organization. You learned to be dependent. You can learn to be independent.

The New Contract

Two statements summarize the new psychological contract between you and your employer:

- Security is your own responsibility.
- The customer knows best.

Career Security Is Up to You

"The biggest mistake you can make," someone once said, "is to think that you work for somebody else." You work for yourself. You sell your skills to the highest bidder. When you begin to see yourself that way, you realize that taking responsibility is a mind-set you must have as you manage your career.

The very best way to create your own security is to liberate your mind, to become psychologically self-employed. Your best chances for career security are to approach work as if you are self-employed and to stay professionally up to date. Whether you work as a contractor, as a temporary, or as the employee of a corporation, know that the only thing your employer guarantees you, besides your paycheck, is an opportunity to solve problems and a chance to continue to learn. Consider yourself loosely affiliated with your company. Longevity is out. Liberation is in.

Rosabeth Moss Kanter, author and Harvard professor, believes that if corporations won't guarantee your employment, they should at least guarantee your employability. We'd amend that statement slightly to put the responsibility on the employee, not the employer. *You* should continually enhance your ability to hold a job. An enlightened employer will emphasize enhanced employability as a major benefit of working for the company. There are a few companies that point out to new employees that experience gained by working for the company will lead employees to a higher level of employability. Does taking on the responsibility for your own self-determined career sound like a lot of work? Do you wonder if you have the skill and the will to manage yourself? You really don't have a choice. The people who will come out ahead are the people who are able to step up to the challenge, accept it, and make the most of it.

Beware of acting out your anger about the change in contracts by saying to yourself, "If I can't count on security, then to heck with working so hard!" or "If I can't climb the ladder, I'll build lousy ladders." These are self-defeating attitudes that will not help you build career security. The trick is to be committed without being consumed, to be committed with no strings attached, to be committed because it's an energizing way to work, not because of a possible payoff down the road. If we can't count on the organization to give us a reason for working, we must find our own reasons. We must figure out, for ourselves, WIIFM (what's in it for me).

When we asked our workshop participants to describe the unwritten agreements that characterize the new contract, here is what they said. Put a check next to any that you currently accept as true, as well as the ones you'd like to cultivate in the future.

- When I am bored, I know it's up to me to find new ways of approaching the job that turn me on.
- I must take responsibility for my career development; the company is no longer in charge of "developing" me.
- As the hierarchy flattens, I have more access to a variety of people throughout the organization. I no longer feel so restricted and hemmed in.
- I have a greater part in decision making.
- Flexibility, versatility, and creativity are appreciated more.
- Taking the initiative is valued rather than looked on with suspicion.
- I have expanded my definition of success and figured out for myself what "quality of worklife" means to me.
- I have more opportunities to direct my learning toward my own career goals.
- I have quit talking about "them," those all-powerful people that run things. Since I can't blame "them" for what's going

on—or not going on—I take more responsibility for solving the problems.
- I have gotten rid of the idea that my career path is carved in stone by the company, and I carve out my own path.
- I have quit looking up at the boss all the time and now focus more on my customers to determine my priorities.
- I have much more anxiety about the future. I have to remember that nobody but me is going to make that future for me.
- I am getting used to partnering with outsiders who are providing services that used to be provided in-house.
- I carefully assess the value to me of rewards beyond possible promotions and pay: flex-time, day care, leave without pay, the chance to learn new skills.
- I have a more objective view of the company. I check out information I receive rather than just accepting it at face value.
- I like having my rewards tied to my individual performance.
- I am more committed to my profession and to developing my expertise than to blindly serving my company.
- I feel like I have more say with my boss about what goes on.
- I am working outside my comfort zone more than ever before.

The Customer Knows Best

Shift your gaze from those above you to those you serve, and you'll take an important step toward forging a new contract with your employer. Organizations no longer have the luxury of hiring people who wait for orders or defer to higher-ups even when they are wrong. Today, the focus is on the market, the customer.

Successful organizations are not reacting to the marketplace but leading it. Paul Zane Pilzer, author of *Unlimited Wealth,* says, "The first law of business is no longer 'find a need and fill it, but imagine a need and create it.' "

Successful organizations are making decisions based on data, not on what management wants. One CEO put it this way: "We have to be fast—like a state-of-the-art camera—so smart about what the customer wants in the future that we can point and shoot with little or no adjustment before the sun goes behind a cloud. That means everybody has to pull their own weight and exercise their own well-honed judgment, instead of trying to impress me by sending me a report with data that's two weeks old already and asking me to decide everything."

Successful organizations are realizing that they can no longer afford to stifle employee input. We've seen the tragedies that happen when employees are not respected partners in decision making and the lines of communication break down. The final "go" in the tragic launching of the Challenger space shuttle was opposed by at least seven key managers and engineers. These skilled professionals could not make their concerns rise up the chain of command to stop the launch.

Successful companies are contracting for employees' high performance, productivity, creativity, flexibility, versatility, and commitment to customers.

Ideally, in this new environment, successful employees can expect to receive not security but opportunity, excitement, a chance to master new skills, and a chance to find meaning in their work as part of a team with a goal they helped to set.

Put Your New Contract to Work

Nobody has to sign your new contract. To put it into action, you simply begin to act as if it has been ratified. You may run into some resistance from yourself.

Intellectually, you might be able to convince yourself that the new agreements make sense. They might even awaken some excitement in you. The organization benefits by increased flexibility and efficiency as it looks for ways to do quality business at the lowest cost. Employees benefit from the chance to use a broader range of skills and to participate more in decision making. In reality, though, you'll probably notice a variety of reactions—not all positive—in yourself and others. Some people react with surprise to the new contract. Some with anger and resentment. Some applaud the changes, seeing different opportunities in the new, unwritten contract. Some aren't aware of the changes yet and are in for a rude awakening. The ten-word slogan on the cover of the product catalog of one of the nation's largest outplacement firms explains why these changes are inevitable: "Because the world is not what it used to be."

Liberating your mind from the old contract and habitual ways of thinking and reacting isn't easy. Here are four steps that will help you move toward psychological self-employment and take control of your career.

Say Good-bye to the Goodies

As you wave good-bye to the old contract, you'll have to give up the goodies of dependency. Oh yes, the old contract had its advantages. You felt secure. You could live under the wing of a big, powerful organization. When somebody asked, "What do you do?" you could always trot out your corporate logo and name drop by saying, "I work for MCI," or "I work for Disney World." Everybody knew where the white lines on the tennis court were. Benefits were bountiful. Perks were plentiful. Progress up the career ladder was inevitable. Somebody else was always there to guide your next step. And somebody was always there to blame if things didn't go well. There were places to hide out for an hour or two, or a day or two, or a year or two, if you didn't feel motivated to work hard just then. You didn't have to ask yourself how you were doing because someone else was responsible for evaluating your contribution and your worth was determined by your salary and title. Somebody else was responsible for everything except what was on your desk, and many of those tasks could only be accomplished after you received approval from someone above you.

You can expect to discover little pockets of dependency in your thinking every so often, even as you are feeling very successful in your quest to become independent and psychologically self-employed. As you recognize what a deep desire people have to be taken care of, you may be amused at your inconsistency.

Mary was trying to convince her ten-year-old, basketball-playing son that it was time for him to learn how to do his own laundry. "When you're on your own you'll need to know how to take care of your clothes, how to cook, how to keep your house clean," Mary said.

"No, mom," her son Brian replied. "When I'm playing for the Chicago Bulls, you and dad can come and live in my mansion with me."

In one part of his head, Brian was an independent, mansion-owning superstar, yet at the same time, he expected Mom to be there to wash his uniforms.

Announce Your New Identity

Put your new contract to work by claiming a new identity: one that reflects your accomplishments, not your association with an admired firm; one that depends on climbing out of the backseat and settling into the driver's seat so that you can steer your own career; one that capitalizes on the connections you make in the professional world rather than one that encourages you to believe that you are just a cog in a complicated machine; one that allows you to derive your self-esteem from who you are and what you do rather than who you work for. An identity that finds the future fascinating, not frightening.

One way to announce your new identity is to come up with a new way of answering the question, "What do you do?" Whenever you meet people—as you introduce yourself at an interdepartmental meeting or at a party—you'll be asked this all-purpose conversation opener. Be ready to introduce yourself in a way that doesn't mention your employer. Just as women no longer introduce themselves in a dependent role, as Mrs. John Smith, for instance, you also can emphasize your independent career identity. Separate yourself from the company that direct deposits your paycheck every two weeks. Instead of saying, "I'm a Business Analyst II with Prudential," you might say, "I streamline the way marketing reports are put together so that agents have vital customer information almost instantly.''

Instead of saying, ''I'm with Pillsbury in Management Information Systems,'' you might explain, ''I help people use new technologies to communicate better. Last week, I finished a videoteleconferencing installation that will allow people in twelve different locations to collaborate on managing projects.''

This kind of introduction teaches people who you are and what you do. It's not that you're trying to hide your company affiliation. It's just that you are refocusing so that the central feature of your career is what you do and what you contribute, not whose logo appears on your business card. Your self-esteem comes from taking pride in your skills and accomplishments more than from basking in the reflected glory of your current employer's name. Avoid merely giving a job title. If you say ''I'm a systems engineer,'' people will say, ''Where?'' And you're back to telling who you work for. People also might be unsure about what that really means and what to talk to you about, and they'll say politely, ''Oh, that's nice.''

There are other benefits of introducing yourself by telling what you do and giving an example of a success. It's a much better conversation starter than saying, ''I work for Bank of America.'' Telling what you do and giving an example of a recent accomplishment teaches people about your skills. If you should be laid off down the road, you've already begun to build your network by teaching people about your character and competence.

Write out several different ways to answer the question, ''What do you do?'' One might be formal. One might be informal or even playful. One might highlight your skills as a manager. Another might show your expertise in a technical area.

Notice what kinds of reactions your newly liberated introductions get from the people you meet. Notice how much easier it is to start conversations when you provide an example of what you do rather than just tell your company name. Notice the feeling of independence you get when you direct attention toward your talents and away from your title.

Take Charge of Your Organizational Identity

Technical workers used to be considered oddballs in many organizational cultures because they identified more with their professions than with the organizations they worked for. It's not that they didn't work hard. On the contrary, they were great contributors. It's just that they felt more like engineers than employees of BIGCO. Now, that attitude seems to make more and more sense.

What would you like your reputation in the organization to be? What would you like to be known for? What are your professional goals and how could they dovetail with the direction the organization is headed? What projects would you like to work on? What new skills would you like to learn? Whom would you like to have for a mentor? What kind of support would you like from your boss as you direct your career? Answering these questions and acting on your decisions will help you make unique contributions in the organization and reduce your psychological dependency on your employer.

The late Soichiro Honda delighted in offering stinging critiques of corporate Japan and the way it controlled the lives of its workers. He said, "Each individual should work for himself—that's important. People will not sacrifice themselves for the company. They come to work at the company to enjoy themselves."

In an otherwise forgettable movie, *A Shock to the System,* star Michael Caine is being questioned by a policeman who asks, pointing to a man across the room, "Is he your superior?" Caine replies, "No, he's my boss." Realize that if you grant to your boss a superior status, you must take on an inferior status. You can acknowledge a boss's authority without giving up your own.

A few people have known this all along. Robert Davidson, a communications professional with Chesapeake and Potomac Telephone Company of Washington, D.C. was ahead of his time when he wrote this poem in the 1950s.

Your Boss*

Whom do you work for? The Boss? Ah, no!
He merely points you the way to go—
He sets up the tasks that you're hired to do—
But he isn't really the boss of YOU.

Whom do you work for? The Boss of the Boss?
The Company handing your pay across?
You owe them the best that you have, 'tis true,
But neither one claims to be boss of YOU.

Whom do you work for? Yourself, my friend—
From morning's light till the day's dark end—
And the boss that you finally answer to
Is nobody else in the world but YOU!

As your career unfolds and as the market drives the formation of more flexible corporate structures, we predict you'll discover a future in which it will be more and more possible for your boss to become your partner.

Here are several more ways to take charge of your organizational identity and act more like an independent contributor, not an employee.

- Negotiate your severance package when you are hired and be sure to update the agreement at the time of your annual review. As with salary, the best time to discuss this is after you've been offered the job. Ask what previous packages have included. Find out if severance packages are tied to grades or to years of service or to other criteria.
- Take an active role in your performance evaluation. Prepare a list of accomplishments. Include awards, degrees, certifications, or accreditations you've earned outside the organization, too. Be proactive in setting goals with your boss.

*By Robert Davidson; used with permission of his grandson, Tom Davidson.

Look for ways to align your own career-building needs and wants with the customer-serving needs of your organization.

- Write your own career plan. Include skills you want to learn and how you'll learn them. Find mentoring relationships inside and outside the organization. Initiate learning projects that will ensure your career security down the road, even if you leave your current employer. Take advantage of tuition assistance and in-house courses to keep current in job-related skills and to explore adjacent areas in case your division, department, or function disappears.
- Get to know people at all levels and in different areas of your organization. Faith Popcorn, who studies future trends and how they'll affect our work, has good advice for us. She says whatever you need to know, whatever your challenge is, the answer is *not* in your office. The answer is in someone else's head. Use inside networking to bash bureaucratic bottlenecks and get the job done fast. Sometimes people think that if you're networking, you're only schmoozing on company time. Help others in your organization see the value of networking, the value of building strong relationships that provide information, resources, and support.

Look for Life Outside Your Organization

To create a career that is less dependent on your current employer, "get a life," as the teenagers say. Here are a few ways to develop a professional and personal identity separate from your current employer.

- Give 10 percent of your own time to yourself. Decide what activity will bring you the most career security and personal growth. A membership in a health club so you can keep your youthful energy and form? Professional association work so you can connect with others in your field? A volunteer activity so you can interact with a diverse group of people from the entire community?
- Get your own business card printed up—one that doesn't give your current employer's name. Why? Your sense of professional independence and entrepreneurial adventure

will be heightened. Suppose you're at a conference and uncover a small consulting job that does not involve a conflict of interest with your employer. In this situation, you'll want a card to give to your potential client. That card should highlight your skills, not your current employer. Jerri works for a large electric utility as a quality facilitator, but she has another card that gives her name and says, "Management Trainer." She uses this card when she talks with small companies that might use her services.

- Develop an outside source of income. Teaching, writing, speaking, and consulting are natural ways for white-collar workers to branch out. Not only can you build up your freedom fund should you be laid off or decide to move on, but you also will feel more psychologically self-employed as you begin to earn some money on your own. The amount isn't important, at least initially. What counts is that you have a professional identity that is separate from the paycheck you earn from your employer.
- Seek out others who are psychologically self-employed. The quality of our lives is largely determined by the company we keep. Get away from people who are still playing "Ain't it awful." Avoid people who, when talking about their boss or employer are stuck in "You won't believe what *they've* done now!" Find people in your organization and out in the world who are excited, creative, upbeat, and supportive.

Claim the Benefits of the Win/Win Contract

What do you and your organization gain by creating a more adult-to-adult relationship to replace the old superior/subordinate relationship? On the organization's side, the impetus may have come from no longer being able to offer job security due to upheavals in markets and the economy. Organizations also realize that employees who are liberated from the dependency trap of the old contract and all the passivity, lack of personal responsibility, and avoidance of accountability it implies, have the potential to be more productive, creative, and flexible. They can make more substantial contributions to the bottom line.

On the employee side, the new contract offers more opportunities for self-expression through work, more chances to explore your changing interests, and more possibilities to adapt work to your lifestyle needs. Becoming psychologically self-employed means believing that you are an independent worker who is leasing your talents to the most attractive bidder and who is defining what you want in return. It means taking assignments based on your life and career goals, as well as on the company's needs. In fact, everybody wins.

As the Company Gets . . .	**You Get . . .**
High performance	Opportunities for mastery
Commitment	The ability to contribute your best
Productivity	A track record of demonstrable competence in your field
Innovation	The excitement of being creative
Competitiveness in world market	Accomplishments for your resumé
Flexibility	Increased ability to adapt and change

Part of accepting the new contract means recognizing that balancing the benefits of dependence with the glories of being on our own has always been an issue. As children and as students we long for more freedom and autonomy, yet enjoy the feeling of being taken care of. Our parents and teachers take pride in our increasing abilities and independence, but like it when we say, "Yes, sir" and follow their advice. When we become adults, the organizations we work for also encourage individual initiative but may subtly discourage us from becoming too independent.

To get clear on what you'd like your new psychological contract to include, read these examples, written by people in our workshops.

Mary's Contract
I Am Psychologically Self-Employed

I have a day-to-day contract with my company to use my services. When the contract is no longer mutually beneficial, I will look for other opportunities, rather than waiting for "them" to shape up. I acknowledge that there is no more "they." I choose to see myself as the major player in my relationship with my employer. I will negotiate rather than accept and placate. I will tell the truth as I see it about my needs and interests rather than trying to fit into other's expectations of where my career should go.

I will continually test out my marketable skills by interviewing for other jobs. When people ask me, "What do you do?" I will not let myself off the hook by simply responding with the name of my prestigious company. Instead, I will say what I do and teach people about my skills. I will put who I currently work for in the proper perspective.

Dan's Contract
My New Contract

1. In the past fourteen years, I have been assigned six different jobs at four different locations in my company. *I* will choose my next assignment.
2. I will take more risks, rather than trying to accommodate and blend in.
3. I am willing to leave the company if I can't find an assignment here that excites me.
4. I've decided that, although I would welcome a promotion, I will measure my success at work by how alive I feel, by how much I'm learning, and by how much I'm able to contribute.
5. I choose to work here. It's not a sacrifice. It's not because of my mortgage or my wife or my status needs. It's not, "I have to go to work." I choose to work here.

Nancy's Contract
No More Namby-Pamby, Nicey-Nicey

I realize I've been tiptoeing through my work life, acting small and meek. No more!

I will stand up and make my voice heard. In staff meetings, I know I'm prepared, so I will take the risk of speaking first, not last. I will stop worrying about making waves and sticking out. I will trust that honesty is the best policy and that it's my duty to tell it like I see it. I will tell my boss what my career goals are and explain how she can help me to reach them, while I make my contribution to the organization.

I will reclaim my life outside of work by reserving more time and energy for professional and personal pursuits. I will invest in my career security by getting a master's degree in the field of my choice, not restricting myself to areas that my company is willing to pay for. I will be aware that, even if the company pays for the degree, the expertise belongs to me.

I will actively build my relationships with people who seem to be comfortable with this new kind of contract. I will let go of the past and move on, even if it means spending less time with old friends who are still into being negative about it all.

Remind yourself that under the new rules of the game, you always work for yourself even though you get a paycheck from your company. You look for problems to solve and lease your skills, your time, and your loyalty to the highest bidder. You give your loyalty and creativity to the organization that offers the most of whatever is important to you right now: an especially interesting or challenging assignment, a specific salary, a benefits package, valued training, a schedule to your liking, the chance to work with a respected leader in the field, or whatever else constitutes quality of work and life to you. In return you get not job security for life but the opportunity to contribute and the freedom to manage your own career.

As you rewrite your unwritten contract, you liberate your mind. You're implementing the first survival strategy and are on your way toward fireproofing your career.

Chapter 7

Line Up Your Finances

Money. That's the first thing that leaps into people's minds when they hear the words, "Sorry. We have to lay you off."

They think, "How will I ever pay the mortgage?" or "Oh no. My son's college tuition is due in three weeks," or "Why did I ever let my credit card bills get so high?"

Losing your paycheck, even for a few months, can be devastating if you haven't prepared yourself financially.

If you have a head-in-the-sand, things-will-be-better-tomorrow approach to your finances, it probably showed up in your answers to the quiz in chapter 1. Those few questions on our quiz that focus on your financial preparedness can't begin to cover everything you should be doing, however. Now, while you're still employed, is the time to analyze your financial security and create your fireproof protection plan.

With a good plan, if you do get laid off, you'll be able to devote your energy and creativity to reestablishing your career, not coping with your creditors.

The Way We Were

For many people, money has never been a problem that time couldn't solve. The expanding economy and the tradition of upward mobility almost guaranteed periodic raises. If these people did any financial planning, it was short-term. It focused on belt-tightening (spending less on entertainment) or postponing (waiting another six months to buy a new car). They believed, and rightly so, that if they simply waited, things would get better.

You can't bank on the future anymore. People used to be able to do just that. They spent their raises before they got them. Hal says, "I used to buy a new car every other year—a more expensive one each time—counting on my 6 percent raise to help me make the payments."

Nita confesses, "I knew I couldn't really afford my house payments, but I talked my dad into helping me for the first year. My argument to him was that I'd be getting a big raise. But my company gave only token raises last year. I got 1 percent. I had to take a second job just to pay my mortgage."

In the 1970s and early 1980s, when the economy was growing, the need to take charge financially was lower on the list of essential life skills. Not so in the 1990s. "Any era can be described as 'uncertain,' but this one more than most," writes Jane Bryant Quinn, author of *Making the Most of Your Money: Smart Ways to Create Wealth and Plan Your Finances in the '90s.* "The error of the 1980s," she says, "was to jump without a parachute. The wisdom of the 1990s is always to know where the ripcord is."

When you contemplate being laid off and losing your paycheck for an extended period of time, you'll realize that it's time to take more drastic measures to protect yourself.

Your Money Mentality

You may find the financial aspect of fireproofing challenging because of the stuff you have in your head about money—

your money mentality. Attitudes about money will either limit or expand your ability to act creatively, especially in times of crisis.

Crisis planning is best done ahead of the crisis. Vow to create and implement your plan now, before a layoff strikes. Your plan will help you avoid panic and the bad decisions that panic begets.

Being prepared financially to weather a layoff can help you avoid making major career mistakes that will impact your earning power for the rest of your life. A study by Drake, Beam and Morin Inc., an outplacement consulting firm, reports that 41 percent of the job hunters that firm surveyed took jobs at a lower salary; 34 percent got an increase, and the rest had no change in pay. Another survey (one we've already mentioned) indicated that only one-fourth of those who found reemployment were able to hang on to their previous salaries. One interpretation of these statistics has to be that the people who took jobs at lower salaries were stampeded into doing so because they didn't have the financial staying power to wait until they found the right job at the right pay. They needed to make some money immediately. By evaluating and improving your financial base now, you'll be able to resist saying "Yes" too early in your job hunt to that financially insufficient offer.

What mysteries, myths, and mind-sets hold you back from managing money effectively and, consciously or unconsciously, influence your financial decisions? As you read, consider your own barriers or mental blocks to taking charge of your financial future. Talk them over with your spouse, family, and friends.

The Mystery

Me? Talk about money? By the time you were ten years old, you probably got the message: "It's not nice to talk about the M-word."

Money has replaced sex as the number one taboo topic. People eagerly chat about the well-publicized, out-of-sight salaries of CEOs and ballplayers, but clam up when money talk gets personal. As adults, if we talk about financial successes, we feel like we're bragging. If we talk about our failures, we feel embarrassed. If we talk about our uncertainties, we feel like dummies, stupid and vulnerable. Because we don't talk about money, we have no benchmarks to tell us how well or how badly we're doing.

In many families, money matters are discussed behind closed doors. Asking about money in your family may be considered rude, at best, and greedy, at worst. In some families, there's still a "father knows best" attitude toward money. It's something that women and children shouldn't "worry their pretty little heads about." However, when you anticipate a radical change in your financial situation, the best thing you can do is to talk with your immediate and extended family about the possibility of your being laid off. Talk over options and alternatives. Could family members provide any assistance? This conversation may be difficult, but you need to know if you can or cannot count on some help, and what kind, and for how long.

With friends, we're more likely to discuss affairs of the heart than matters of the checkbook. Does your best friend know how much you make? Financial specifics are often considered off limits, even among the best of friends.

In the workplace, salaries, bonuses, and benefits are often shrouded in silence. Employees are warned not to discuss them. We perpetuate these mysteries by not talking with colleagues.

It's hard to understand why the M-word is taboo in the workplace. Unless there are unexplainable inconsistencies, why should management care if people know how much their coworkers make? Unfair salary discrepancies among employees who have similar jobs are encouraged by people's reluctance to share information. Unless their pay is hard to justify, why would managers care if subordinates know the amount of management paychecks? Pay equity is one part of the employee/employer relationship that people care passionately about. We want salaries to be fairly distributed. That's reasonable. Why the big mystery?

Beth made the following entry in her journal.

> After a long, hard battle for increased salaries, our Friday paychecks reflected a "pittance" raise. No one said anything positive, like, "Good job." No one said anything negative either, like, "You don't deserve this." There was no communication about the raise one way or another. Out of about 100 employees, only seven of us got raises.
>
> Two employees were directly told not to discuss these raises because "not everyone received one." Because of the secrecy regarding salaries, much distrust has been created. Finances are held to be confidential information and seem to set employee against employee and employee against employer. All of these secrets decrease the level of communication within the company.
>
> It seems to me that salary ranges and explanations of merit raises should be common knowledge for employees. Honesty and education only increase growth and trust within any system, whether that be a family unit or a corporation. People have to know their responsibilities and what is expected of them. Without these guidelines, confusion and chaos follow. In our case, the small bridge of company loyalty between the employees and the employer collapsed. Many people felt used. Some have reacted with anger, and some say, "Don't get mad—get even." None of these reactions is good for this company.

As long as money remains a secret—at home or in the workplace—it can't be managed effectively. Exploring beliefs, sharing information and strategies, developing money management skills, and seeking advice is exactly what is necessary to take the mystery out of the M-word.

We shy away from discussions of money because of the subtle but pervasive and powerful equations we make about its meaning.

The Myths

Money is a loaded subject. Deep down, most people believe salaries, savings, and spending are an index of their self-worth. You are what you make. You are what you have. You are what you spend. Deepak Chopra, stress management expert and author of *Quantum Healing,* says, "Most people find it extremely difficult to tell someone exactly how much money they make. . . . They believe at the gut level of emotion that they are worth only what they earn."

People wrestle with the questions: How much should I learn? Am I worth it? But, what you get paid has nothing to do with your worth and everything to do with market value. You get paid what the market says you should get paid. The market sometimes makes strange decisions, such as when garbage collectors earn more than school teachers, for example.

As you become conscious of your beliefs—the myths you buy into—think about how they might trigger nonproductive actions in times of stress. Do any of the equations listed below govern your relationship with money?

- *Money is happiness.* "If I buy something new, I'll feel better." Somebody once said, "What good is happiness? You can't buy money with it." That's a clever twist on an old idea. Many people do equate money with happiness. If you learned as a child that spending money is the way to lift depression, you might revert to buying-spree behaviors even though, when you're thinking maturely, you know that the worst time to pile up credit card debt or dip into your savings account is when layoff rumors are flying.
- *Money is love.* "If I buy an expensive gift, she will know how much I care." At work, someone might think, "If I am well-paid, I am well-liked and my work is appreciated."
- *Money is self-esteem.* "I'm of value because I have a job that pays me well." For many people salary and self-esteem are inseperable.

- *Money is success.* "If I have a high paying job, I'm successful."
- *Money is power.* "If I have money, I'll be able to call the shots."
- *Money is freedom and independence.* "If I have money, I'll be free to do what I want." In reality, the insistance on using money as a measurement restricts freedom and tethers people to jobs they dislike.
- *Money is security.* "If I have money, I'll be safe." The best safety is to know you have—and to constantly demonstrate to yourself—the ability to keep on generating income, no matter what comes.

Though all of these beliefs contain some elements of truth, equating money with any of these concepts makes rational decision making about finances impossible.

Men and women approach the topic of money differently. One research study found that men associate money with happiness, excitement, respect, love, and reverence. Women, on the other hand, associate money with anxiety, depression, anger, helplessness, envy, resentment, fear, guilt, panic, sadness, shame, hatred, and spite. Half of the women and one-third of the men had, at some time in their lives felt helpless because of money. What are your associations with money?

Your Mind-set

You may need new beliefs about money.

Before tackling the very necessary tasks of adding up your assets, totaling your liabilities, and planning your budget, spend time on this three-step process for developing a conscious and creative relationship with money.

Step One: Jot down your observations and thoughts about money. Record your worries, assumptions, beliefs, judgments, and what your family taught you. Becoming conscious of these thoughts will alert you to the myths that influence your money management, will reopen your options, and will guide you as you make new choices about your money mind-set. Recording thoughts about money often reveals outdated ideas and unsubstantiated assumptions. Because many of our beliefs about how the world operates and our place in it are developed when we're little kids, and these ideas are never questioned again, deciding to get conscious about your money mind-set can give you renewed power and insight when it comes to developing creative, sensible responses to a financial crisis like a layoff. Here are some questions to ask yourself:

- What did my parents think about making and spending money? How are my beliefs similar or different?
- What do I think is the most money I'll ever make in a year? Where did that figure (my psychological salary ceiling) come from? Why?
- What career and job decisions have I made because of money? What price have I paid for those decisions? What were the pros and cons of those decisions?
- What is my "dollar threshold" (the amount I spend without planning, thinking, budgeting, or checking with my spouse)?

After writing about money in her journal for two weeks, Monica said, "I realized the six-year-old inside of me was controlling my beliefs and decisions about money. I was acting out of fear rather than out of trust in myself as a competent, creative adult."

Step Two: Talk to people about money. Find people you trust and talk with them about everything from purchasing decisions to different types of investments, the best place to shop, how to make the most from your garage sale, and the name of a competent financial planner.

Many money decisions we have to make today are complicated, require some research, and involve specialized terminology. It's time we banded together and pooled our resources, like the two friends who discovered that they both were in the market for a new car and both were researching how to find scholarship aid for their college-age children. They decided to divvy up the research and meet again in a week to share information and resources.

Although each of us will decide what feels appropriate, here's a list of people you might talk to and some questions or topics you might bring up.

- *With your spouse:* "If I lost my job in six months, how could we begin now to cut expenses and save more?"
- *With a friend:* "How do you go about budgeting and planning?"
- *With a sibling:* "Let's talk about what financial decisions we need to make now so that mom's transition to the retirement home creates the largest possible pool of money for her."
- *With a financial advisor:* "I may be laid off in the next eight or nine months. What should I do now to protect my assets?"
- *With a mentor or boss:* "Let's sit down sometime and go over the pros and cons of this new medical plan."
- *With your children:* "We're on a very tight budget this year, so I won't be able to buy you a new bike, but I will help you make flyers to advertise your lawn-mowing service so you can earn the money to buy one."

Step Three: Write out your own "money manifesto." Your manifesto should be a short statement that describes how you choose to view and use money. Here are two examples.

Laura's Money Manifesto

My money will be my servant, not my master. I will seek financial independence to every extent possible. My wants will be subject to my needs and my means. Except for my mortgage and occasional car loans, I will keep myself free from consumer debt. I will spend less than I earn, regularly tithe a tenth, and invest a tenth of my income before taxes.

Julian's Money Manifesto

I am not my salary. The money I earn is not an indication of my self-worth. Expressions of caring and time spent together are better indications of my love for my family and friends than buying something with an expensive price tag. Spending time with my kids is more important to me than working late to earn more so I can buy them expensive toys or clothes. I will establish clear agreements with my employer about the hours I work.

Many of the plans people need to put into place have no particular deadline, so they put off developing a conscious and comprehensive financial strategy until tomorrow. Watching hardworking, high-performing friends and colleagues who have been laid off struggle as they try to deal with a financial crisis on top of a career crisis is the closest thing to a wake-up call you'll get.

Where You Are

To create the maximum career security for yourself, financial muddling is out. Financial management is in. Begin by determining where you stand, financially.

Collect Your Data

You'll need to have a variety of documents handy to perform your financial analysis, including:

- A financial statement form (available from your bank)
- A copy of your most recent income tax documents
- Your employee benefits handbook
- Information about your stock plans, 401(k), and other savings
- Credit card bills for the last year
- Canceled checks for the last year

- Insurance information, including home, car, life, and disability insurance
- Information about outstanding loans (car, mortgage, school, home equity)

Assess Your Situation

Complete the financial statement form. It is a summary of your assets and liabilities—what you own and what you owe. Your goal is to get down on paper a complete picture of what you own and owe, so that you can see what you need to work on.

Add Up Your Assets: Are there things you could sell for immediate cash if you need to raise money? How much cash? How about stocks, real estate, jewelry, antiques, or coin collections? Are there other assets that you may not have thought to list? How much money would they bring if you could sell them? Are there items you could borrow against, such as paid-up insurance policies?

Determine the availability (accountants call it the liquidity) of your money. Check out how easily you could convert various assets to cash. Make notes to remind yourself how long it would take to get at the money represented by your assets.

Are you taking maximum advantage of your current benefits? Explore your employee benefits handbook to find out. Look for information on savings plans, stock plans, 401(k) plans, before-tax reimbursement accounts, and tuition assistance, for example.

List Your Liabilities: How can you reduce them? After separating out your mortgage, add up the total amount you owe.

It makes sense to figure out ways to reduce your monthly expenses in preparation for a period of time during which you might be without a paycheck. Your mortgage is probably your largest single monthly expenditure, so it makes sense to work on whittling it down first. Could you refinance to lower your monthly payments? Research the cost of refinancing by talking to banks and mortgage brokers. What would it cost? How much could you save? Of course, if you are not laid off, you can speed up your mortgage payments by prepaying principal.

Have you already taken out a home equity loan? How fast can you pay it off so that you can list your line of credit as an asset rather than a liability? If you have an unused line of credit on your home equity, you could borrow against it and use that money to tide you over. If you do not have a home equity loan, consider getting one set up, borrowing the maximum against it, and depositing the money in another bank or money market fund. Some lenders will not extend you a line of credit after you are laid off because they base their decisions to lend money on your income.

Look at other debts. How can you reduce or eliminate them? What would you do if you were laid off? Could you sell items you are still paying for such as your car, your boat, or your motor home? How fast could you do that? What are the items worth? How do you know? Assign priorities to various items that you are still paying for and determine now, while your mind is clear, what you best could do without.

Determine Your Income and Expenses: On one piece of paper, write down all income. Be sure you use the real figure after subtracting deductions such as taxes, health insurance, FICA, etc. Include any additional income from dividends, interest, rents, etc.

On another page, list yearly expenses and periodic expenses (such as car insurance).

On a third page, list your monthly expenses. Begin your monthly expense list with the largest figure, probably your mortgage, and list other expenses in descending order. You may need to use your canceled checks or check register to get a handle on these. (If you have been writing checks at the grocery store that are larger than the total on your register tape, you may need to do some intensive record keeping for a couple of months to determine your real cost of groceries and the amounts of money you take in cash to pay incidentals.) Average a year's worth of electric bills, gas bills, and gasoline credit card bills, to get an average monthly cost for these basic bills.

Circle all expenses that are vital. Is there any way to reduce them? Your electric and gas companies probably perform free audits, for example, to show you ways to reduce your use. One family found that they could save nearly $500 a year by replacing incandescent bulbs with fluorescents in only half the lights in their house.

Add up your bare bones monthly expenses to determine how much money you need to live on. Multiply that number by twelve to figure out how big a financial reserve you would need to cover a year-long job hunt. (Remember that it takes many people more than twelve months to find a new job. Also remember that only 25 to 40 percent of white-collar job hunters find jobs that pay the same or better than the ones they lost. You don't want to be stampeded into taking a job at a much lower salary because you don't have the staying power for a long job hunt.)

Most people are stunned by the amount they will need to live on. Check the items you included as vital. Do you really need cable TV?

Another way to categorize your monthly expenditures is to divide them into three groups: fixed (rent, mortgage, car payments, utilities), flexible (food, clothing, education), and frills (entertainment, club memberships, vacations). Remember, even some of the fixed expenses can be lowered and some items in the flexible category could be bumped back to frills.

Note that some expenses might decrease if you were laid off, business lunches and downtown parking, for example. However, you will have new expenses during your job hunt: resumé preparation, mailing, telephone, career counseling, health insurance, and memberships in professional associations if they previously were paid for by your employer. Investigate and then estimate these possible expenses so you can include them in your post-layoff budget.

Learn about Severance, Benefits, and Unemployment: Don't assume that all your needs will be met by severance pay and unemployment benefits. The dependent employee approaches the possibility of a layoff thinking, "What are they going to do for me?" The psychologically self-employed person says, "What can I do to take care of myself and my family?"

Consult your employee handbook to see if the company has spelled out a standard severance policy. If not, you may need to talk to people who have previously been laid off to determine what you are likely to get and for how long. Some organizations provide one year's salary, others one week's salary for each year worked. Most will pay you for unused vacation time. Some will pay for unused sick days. Sometimes it's tough to get answers about severance since companies may change their policies from one layoff to the next.

Employees may be told not to discuss the details of their severance package. After Laurie was laid off, she told an acquaintance that she had signed a legal document prohibiting her from telling anyone what she received. Several years after she was laid off, Laurie says the reason she believes she was prohibited from talking about what she got was that the company had no policy at all and so they probably decided that the safest thing to do was swear her to silence.

Another reason that it's tough to get information is that different levels in the organization may be offered different packages. After Doris was laid off, she found out that if her job had been rated one point higher in the company's job rating system, she would have been eligible for twice as much severance pay.

Severance pay is only part of the picture. Check out your current health insurance coverage. If you have a working spouse, be sure you are enrolled now in *both* plans. You should know that employers with more than twenty workers must allow you to continue your health insurance for some period of time, but you will have to pay the cost. Determine what that cost would be and add that number to your bare bones monthly expense budget.

Lester almost opted for a lump sum distribution of his severance pay. Then he found out that his company-paid health insurance would stop when he received his last severance payment. He decided to choose a payout plan that spread out his severance pay over the longest time period possible to keep his health insurance in force as long as possible.

Find out how much you would be entitled to in unemployment benefits from your state. A phone call to your local office will provide you with some ballpark information about how much you could receive, how to apply, what you have to do to qualify and to register, how soon payments would begin, and how long they would continue. Don't be lulled into a false sense of security by thinking, "Oh, I'll have unemployment." Get the facts. By the way, if you say that you are starting your own business, you are not entitled to unemployment benefits because it is assumed that you are not available to actively seek a new job.

Get Expert Advice

You may need some advice from an expert. We recommend that you find a fee-only financial planner. Make sure you feel comfortable with that person and are confident that he or she has the expertise you need. Here are some questions to ask when interviewing a financial planner or advisor.

- What areas does your financial planning service include (goal-setting, tax planning, managing monthly expenses, budgeting, choosing an investment strategy, assessing insurance needs, determining liquidity of assets)?
- Can you help me think through creative alternatives and create a safety net to minimize the impact of a short-term or long-term interruption of my income?
- What degrees and certifications have you earned?
- How are you compensated (fee only, commissions only, fee and commissions, or fee offset)?
- Will you provide references from past and present clients?

Your accountant, lawyer, insurance agent and banker are sources of information, too. Also, don't forget people you know who have already been through a layoff. Ask their advice and what they wish they'd done differently to prepare financially.

Create Your Plan

Construct a budget and a plan that will accomplish your objectives:

- Create a financial reserve or know how you will raise the money sufficient to cover bare bones living expenses for one year.
- Prevent new debt and reduce old debt.
- Increase your income.

There are only three things you can do about money: spend less, earn more, and/or manage better.

To Spend Less: Remember the Depression-era motto: ''Use it up, wear it out, make it do, or do without.'' The words *thrift* and *thrive* come from the same old Norse word that means prosperity.

To Earn More: Consider moonlighting, self-employment, and the big three moneymakers, consulting, teaching, or writing. This tactic will

- Add new dimensions and skills to your resumé
- Reduce your dependence on your core employer and build confidence about your ability to continue to create income
- Help you learn about record keeping and taxes, in case you want to work for yourself during a period of unemployment or go into business for yourself
- Provide tax deductions for business setup and home office equipment
- Allow you to put 15 percent of your annual self-employed income into a Keogh plan or a simplified employee pension plan and get a tax deduction for it

To Manage Better: Make a list of your monthly expenses. Beginning with the largest expense, design a reduction plan. Become a savvy spender—even a penny pincher.

• • •

The following examples come from people who attended our workshops and then went to work on their finances. Their plans and our commentaries on their decisions will provide some ideas for you.

Gil and Rashena

Gil, forty-six, is a sales and marketing manager. His wife Rashena, forty-three, is not employed outside the home. They have two children, ages fourteen and eighteen.

"It was right before Thanksgiving," Gil remembers. "It was like living on the side of a volcano. There were constant rumbles about a merger—and layoffs to get rid of the excess people. I remember thinking for the first time in my eighteen-year career, 'I could get laid off.' I couldn't get the thought out of my mind. 'I could get laid off.' It had nothing to do with my performance. I was in shock during the holiday weekend, mulling over this new idea, testing it out, looking for loopholes through which to escape the awful truth. But there it was, over and over again: 'I could get laid off.' What had happened to strangers in the newspapers, neighbors down the street, my cousin in Cincinnati, could happen to me.

"At first, when I woke up to my here today, gone tomorrow relationship with my employer, I didn't know what to do with this newfound insight. With one child starting college and another starting high school, some of my most financially demanding years were yet to come. But my fear fueled action. After going to a Fireproof workshop, I talked with Rashena, my wife. We decided to take a hard look at our finances. We spent several evenings examining monthly expenses. We decided to hire a certified financial planner to help us assess our financial health and look at options. We immediately cut spending. We'd been playing with a money-making idea and decided to get serious about it. Rashena, who has a degree in English, had done volunteer work with various civil rights organizations for years. If I do get laid off, she could look for a paid job. Because of her volunteer work, she's a whiz on the computer. We feel much more in control now that we have taken the first steps to take a more active role in managing our finances."

Gil and Rashena's Decisions

Spend Less

1. House swap with friends in Denver for our vacation, rather than staying in a hotel. Drive rather than fly. Savings: $3,000.
2. Delay plans to buy a third car for our sons to use. Savings: $5,000, plus gas, maintenance, and insurance.
3. Join a discount food club. Buy in bulk. Eat lower on the food chain and eliminate pricey snack foods and most liquor.
4. Instead of replacing my worn-out riding lawn mower, propose to a good neighbor that we buy a mower together. If that idea doesn't work out, buy a push mower and pat myself on the back for getting more exercise!

Earn More

1. Help college-age son apply for scholarships and grants. Think we can get at least $1,500.
2. Hold garage sale to get rid of unused items collected over the last ten years. Estimated profit: $700. And going through the junk will be an exercise in learning and hopefully avoiding future impulse buying of gadgets and stuff as we confront our bad buys of the decade.
3. Self-publish a 100-page booklet on local children's camps and how to evaluate them. Rashena has just about completed this booklet. Projected income: $3,000.

Manage Better

1. Refinance house to cut monthly payments by at least $100 a month.
2. Establish a home equity line of credit and *don't use it,* in case cash is needed. Estimated line of credit: $23,000.
3. Begin working with certified financial planner to look at short-term and long-term management of assets.

Commentary on Gil and Rashena's Decisions

Low overhead equals freedom. Gil and Rashena are using some of the best strategies to lower monthly expenses: cutting mortgage payments and food costs.

Rashena is well-positioned to make a significant financial contribution to the family. Perhaps she should go ahead and enter the job market now, to avoid the stress of possibly having two job-seekers in the family at one time.

This couple is smart to establish a relationship with a financial professional. Being willing to invest in expert help pays off in the long run.

Mary Lou

Mary Lou, twenty-eight, is a graphic artist. She is single.

"I graduated from college six years ago and have been working as a graphic artist for an association in Chicago," Mary Lou says. "I never had to look for a job. I went from being a summer intern at the association right into this position.

"I began to get worried when our executive director retired. The new executive reorganized and announced a downsizing. I wasn't hit immediately, but the strategic plan for next year states that all the graphic design will be outsourced. It's a polite way of saying to me, 'Your job is being abolished.' It's quite a shock to look at the new organization chart and not see my job on it.

"For a couple of days, everybody kind of tiptoed around me, wondering whether I would cry, scream, cheer, or leave immediately.

"Finally, my boss called me into his office and said he was sorry that my job was being eliminated and that maybe a job in the membership department would open up. He didn't mention how long I would be employed . . . and I didn't ask. I think he hoped I would quit, but I had a friend in a similar situation who did that and couldn't get unemployment benefits. So, I decided to sit tight and wait to be laid off.

"Meanwhile, I'm taking stock and have decided to make some immediate changes to beef up my skills and downsize my lifestyle. Within six weeks, I will complete every step on my plan. Even if I'm between jobs for a few months, my savings will tide me over."

Mary Lou's Decisions

Spend Less

1. Decrease expenses by $400 a month by moving in with my sister. I'll pay her $200 rent a month. She is recently divorced, so it will help her with her mortgage. Although it's a longer commute to work and I'll spend a little more on gas, my rent will be cut by two-thirds and I'll get to spend more time with my niece and nephew, who are very important to me.
2. Cancel my winter vacation in Jamaica. Savings: $1,600.
3. Control everyday expenses. Every Monday morning, I'll put my spending money (lunches, entertainment, miscellaneous) in a separate envelope in my purse. When the money is gone, I'll take my lunch, find free entertainment, and won't succumb to impulse spending. Savings: $20 a week, $1,040 a year.

Earn More

1. Enroll for a master's degree in marketing, so my expertise is broadened and my long-range earning power is enhanced. At least, I'll get the the first course paid for by my employer's tuition assistance plan.
2. Propose a course in How to Design a Client Newsletter to the noncredit division of the university. Earnings: $400.
3. Look for freelance design opportunities.
4. Check out temporary agencies to see if any of them place graphic design people.

Manage Better

1. Research which credit cards charge the lowest interest. Pay off current balances of $1,900, keep the two cards that charge the lowest interest rates, and get rid of all the others.
2. Take a $55, four-session course in Managing Your Money.

Commentary on Mary Lou's Decisions

If Mary Lou doesn't find a new job quickly, she might take a loan for tuition and go to school full time for a year. The benefit of this backup plan would be that she'd complete her degree more quickly. Perhaps she could lower her living expenses even more by arranging her course schedule so that she could provide after-school care for her niece and nephew in return for rent.

Buying on credit often results in paying three times the purchase price. By reducing or even eliminating credit card debt, Mary Lou, who had nine different credit cards, will save more money than she realizes. It may not be easy for her to get a low-rate credit card: Standards are rigid and 80 percent of those who apply are rejected. Reasons include too much debt, high balances on existing cards, too many cards (including those with zero balances), frequent changes of address, and job hopping. Reformed credit card junkies suggest the following: To quit using your credit cards, freeze them in a gallon jug of water. Then you'll have the time it takes to defrost them to think about whether you really want to use them or not. Another suggestion is to stash the cards in your safety deposit box to put them out of reach.

Mary Lou's decision to take a money management course is a smart move. She knows that financial management is not her strong suit and that, in the long run, ignorance can be more expensive than education.

Mary Lou hasn't mentioned what she will do about health insurance if she gets laid off. How long will her company pay? If she elects to take her severance pay over a longer time, rather than in a lump sum, will that extend her health coverage? Should she sign up for continuing coverage for eighteen months under COBRA (Consolidated Omnibus Budget Reconciliation Act of 1985)? She'll have to pay the entire cost of the premium plus an extra 2 percent for administrative expense. Would she be better off getting insurance through the university where she is getting her master's?

She hopes a lot of these questions will be answered in her Managing Your Money course.

Mary Lou is handicapped by not having a computer of her own for freelance work. She should investigate how much it would cost to buy the equipment she needs to do her work, especially if she decides to go back to school full time. Her idea about checking out employment through temporary agencies is a good one. She might find part-time work that she could combine with school or, if she is laid off, she could take a full-time temporary assignment until she finds a permanent position.

Jane and David

Jane, thirty-eight, is a management information systems manager. Her husband David is purchasing agent for a pharmaceutical company. They have two children, ages seven and nine.

"I returned to work two years ago after my children reached school age," says Jane. "I imagined I'd be here forever.

"I like the benefits and excitement of working for a large corporation. When the first defense cuts came, business seemed to go on as usual, even though the Navy was one of our main customers. When newspaper headlines announced the next round of cuts in the defense industry, it began to sink in. Around the office, speculation was rampant. Everybody saw his job as essential to the organization. Everybody remembered how hard he worked on the last project. Everybody is saying to himself, 'Surely, it won't be me who is laid off.'

"My husband David's job is secure.

"I pay the bills, so I know that as our salaries have grown, so have our expenditures. There isn't a penny left over at the end of the month. We have no savings to speak of and our families don't have the resources to help us out. If I am out of work for even three months, we will be in serious financial trouble.

"My neighbor has been looking for a new job for eight months. Someone else I know has finally taken a job, but at $12,000 less than he was making before he got laid off.

"We must do something now to ease the shock of what seems inevitable: We will have to live on one paycheck. The scary part is we don't know when it will happen or how long it will go on."

Jane and David's Decisions

Spend Less

1. Cut entertainment expenses. A night out for dinner and movies costs us almost $80 (including the babysitter). Instead of going out three times a month, we'll go out only once. Savings: $160 a month.
2. Move the children from private school to public school this fall. Savings: $8,800.
3. Drop the summer swim club membership. Since the kids are in summer camps and day care, we don't really have time to use it much. Savings: $400.
4. Create a co-op babysitting arrangement with four other couples.
5. Buy kids' clothes at thrift shops, consignment shops, and garage sales.
6. Reduce holiday gift giving. Suggest to extended family that we each draw a name for one adult's gift and one child's gift.

Earn More

1. I can't think of any way to earn more money.

Manage Better

1. Sign us all up on David's medical/dental plans immediately. (We had put the entire family on my medical/dental plans because they provided better coverage at less cost.)
2. Sign up for the medical reimbursement account that allows us to set aside $1,200 a year, tax free, to use for medical or dental expenses that aren't covered by our insurance.
3. Join a professional association to gain access to its job bank and to help me focus my networking and job seeking activities. Cost: $150.
4. Check out what my company's policies are on severance pay and find out what unemployment benefits I can expect so that I know how much money we'll have coming in.
5. Increase our contribution to David's 401(k) to 6 percent.

His company matches the first 6 percent of contributions with fifty cents on the dollar.

6. Consolidate credit card debt (current interest averages 18 percent) and reduce monthly interest paid on debt by taking out a home equity loan (at 10 percent).

Commentary on Jane and David's Decisions

The necessity to curtail their spending makes people mad. They think, "How come I can't have what my parents had? Why can't I spend money like I did in the good old days?" Downsizing your lifestyle is bitter medicine for people raised on the American dream of onward and upward. Jane and David are taking a positive approach.

As the prospect of living on one income becomes more real, Jane and David may decide they can't even afford one night a month on the town. They can find free family entertainment. It makes sense to choose to go through the trauma of trimming now, rather than waiting until they are going through the trauma of termination, as well.

Some 70 to 86 percent of white-collar jobs are found through networking, something that is best done before you are laid off. Jane's plan to join a professional association is a smart one.

Jane and David were surprised to see that they spent $1,900 on gift giving last year. With David's two siblings and Jane's four siblings, plus eight nieces and nephews, things had really gotten out of hand and had become a chore not a pleasure. Their solutions sound like more fun for everybody.

Like many couples, Jane and David couldn't think of a single thing to do to increase their income. With young children and demanding jobs, they have little time to devote to creating extra income. However, they should continue to think about other income opportunities.

Congratulations to Jane and David for thinking ahead to retirement by continuing—and even increasing—their savings in his 401(k) plan. Even in these uncertain times and even though they will not be putting as much in as they could, it makes good sense. Amazingly, fewer than 1 percent of all eligible employees contribute the maximum to their company-offered 401(k) plans. Also, for short-run protection, Jane and David may be able to borrow from their 401(k) should Jane be unemployed for a long time. The younger you are, the more carefully you should plan for retirement. Many employers are phasing out pensions for future retirees.

Using a home equity loan (interest on which is probably tax deductible) to consolidate and pay down credit card debt is a good idea. Some people who are facing layoffs have borrowed the maximum on their home equity and put that money in another bank. If you wait until after you've been laid off, your mortgage lender may not allow you to borrow on your equity.

Jane's assumption that David's job is secure may not be warranted. They should immediately reassess his situation, using the questions to determine the risk of a job that begin on page 37.

Sam

Sam, fifty-four, is vice president of human resources development. He's divorced and has two grown children.

"I can see the writing on the wall," says Sam "I don't like what it says. Four years ago I was promoted from director of training to vice president of HRD. I like my work. I'd like to finish out my next ten years here. But everything's changing. I don't think that will happen. My company was bought out a year ago. There's talk of a merger. We don't even write up new organization charts in pencil. Changing them would use up too many erasers.

"Many positions are redundant. Several of my mentors have left with early retirement packages. Our markets have changed. My salary is probably too high, especially when I notice how many really talented HRD people are looking for work and willing to come in for three-fourths of what I make. So I'm telling myself, 'Wake up and smell the coffee. Practice what you preach and take charge. Hang on as long as you can, but assume that fairly soon you'll be asked to leave or want to leave. You don't know exactly when, but it will happen.' Since my divorce three years ago, I've just been trying to adjust and have put off making some changes that now seem imperative. My plan will definitely help me get financially fireproofed."

Sam's Decisions

Spend Less

1. Sell my four-bedroom house and move to a two-bedroom condo. Give half the profit to my ex-wife, as per our divorce agreement. Use my half for a small down payment on a condominium, put the rest in an easy-to-get-at investment, in case I need ready cash.

Earn More

1. Write an article for a professional magazine. Income: $400.
2. Develop a brochure to promote my independent consulting and training services. Goal: One client a month. Use my accumulated vacation days for my business. Net income: $4,000 this year.
3. Explore the mechanics of operating a home-based business. Talk with the Small Business Administration and look into courses. Estimate costs for fax, answering service, secretarial help, copy machine, etc. Get a business license, if necessary.
4. Hire someone to do an estate sale to get rid of all the stuff I won't need in the condo. Income: $4,000.

Manage Better

1. Choose a financial advisor and assess retirement benefits, health plans, stock plans, 401(k), etc.
2. Estimate the severance package that I might be offered if I am laid off.
3. Limit overtime at work. Remind myself that working longer hours is not going to save my job.
4. Split my mortgage payments into bimonthly payments in order to reduce the total interest paid over the long run.

Commentary on Sam's Decisions

Sam gets bonus points for writing a magazine article, not only because of the boost to his freelance feeling, but also because of the obvious career credibility it provides, should he have to look for a job or decide to freelance full time. Getting published will also give him exposure and position him as an expert.

Sam's got an edge on most employees. If anybody should know or could find out the details of previous severance packages, it would be Sam in the human resources development department, where such decisions are made and administered. This information is very difficult for most employees to get. Our suggestion: Talk with previously laid-off employees.

By choosing to limit his overtime, Sam will avoid the mistake we've heard about so often. One man put it this way: "I worked sixty or seventy hours a week trying to get the jobs of three people done and hoping to show my commitment. I got laid off anyway. My personal life suffered, I neglected my network, and I have enough resentment to fill a football stadium."

Wes Poriotis, head of Wesley, Brown & Bartle, an executive search firm, says, "Tithe 10 percent of your own time to thineself. It could be trade association work, volunteer activity with the well-connected, or an occasional foray into the marketplace to see what you are worth." Do something that enhances your ability to achieve career security.

By paying half of his monthly mortgage fifteen days early, Sam can greatly reduce his long-term interest costs. If you make even one extra mortgage payment a year, you can virtually cut a thirty-year mortgage in half—again, with big savings on interest.

The Bottom Line

Most of us walk around in a financial fog. We haven't built a long-range financial strategy that reflects the fact that sometime in our work life we'll probably get that proverbial pink slip. Now's the time to change all that, to become financially savvy, and to implement well-thought-out plans to protect yourself and your family against the loss—even temporarily—of your paycheck.

Nothing will give you more peace of mind in the present and more flexibility in the future than taking charge of your financial situation now.

Chapter 8

Learn for Mastery

Every weekend, Jeanne jets from Kansas City to her MBA classes at the University of Chicago.

Every morning when Bob starts out on his forty-five-minute commute, he pops an audiotape into his player.

As soon as the flyers hit her in-basket, Leona signs up for in-house training sessions.

Night after night, Carter plugs away at his computer, forcing himself to work through the users' manual until he's thoroughly familiar with everything his new software program can do.

Contrast those active learners—Jeanne, Bob, Leona, and Carter—with these folks.

Lyle is a Navy chief with eighteen years of active duty behind him and a chestful of ribbons, but even his buddies call him ROAD (Retired on Active Duty) behind his back. They know he's just warming the chair seat behind his desk, waiting for retirement.

Jack's an old-timer at a trucking company headquarters. When someone greets him in the hall with a "Hi, how are you?" he says with a sneer, "Waiting for five o'clock."

The word *deadwood* was invented to describe Lyle and

Jack. You probably know someone like them. They're not working; they're doing time. They tuned out and turned off years ago. Now, they're merely going through the motions . . . slowly.

Whose careers are more secure? The answer is obvious. The information explosion, advances in technology, and worldwide competition make constant learning necessary. Lifetime learners will always be ready for whatever comes.

In Wonderland, the Red Queen said to Alice, "Now, *here,* you see, it takes all the running you can do, to keep in the same place. If you want to get somewhere else, you must run at least twice as fast as that!" In the U.S. today, we must run more than twice as fast: not to keep our places, not to get somewhere else, but not to be left behind.

Career security is between your ears. There's no substitute for knowledge—the kind of knowledge that makes you stick out in a field of your peers when you're competing for a job or trying to hand on to one in the midst of downsizing, the kind of knowledge you need to stay market-ready, the kind of knowledge you can carry with you to new jobs or transfer to new career fields.

In today's marketplace, knowledge is your product or service. As you become psychologically self-employed, your knowledge is what you have to sell or contract out temporarily to a succession of employers. The dictionary defines a master as someone who is able to work independently. Note the word *able.* As you acquire knowledge, you are able to work without supervision, even if you still report to a boss and get a paycheck from an employer. Mastery is another route to psychological self-employment.

There are two ways of looking at work. You can regard work as a job to do, or you can look at work as an arena in which to learn and to develop expertise.

Have you ever thought through what it would take to become an expert in your field? You can become one. There's nothing magic about it. All it takes is choosing to focus your effort.

- Study the state of the art in a field and become well-acquainted with the theories of the great thinkers and the principles that have been developed by your predecessors.
- Develop a repertoire of special skills or knowledge in a particular field.
- Practice enough to apply those skills easily and adapt them to new circumstances.
- Invest the time it takes to become an authority by virtue of your broad and deep experience.
- Receive high marks on your work from other people in your field.
- Take knowledge one step forward, going beyond the known into the unknown, to create new combinations of ideas and new words to describe those inventions.
- Share your expertise through mentoring, networking, teaching, speaking, writing, and consulting.

The arguments for choosing the road to mastery rather than the path of least resistance are compelling. Have you noticed any experts in your field wandering around talking vaguely about being a career transition and asking, "Do you know of any job openings . . . anywhere?" Experts make more money than run-of-the mill employees. Look around your own career field. Who are the spokespeople, the leaders, the movers and shakers? What kinds of careers do they have? Often experts have multifaceted careers that culminate in sharing their expertise through teaching or consulting or writing.

You don't have to be a genius to become an expert, but you do have to focus your efforts to achieve mastery in whatever you do. Here are the steps to mastery.

- Determine what you need to learn.
- Discover how and where to learn it.
- Draft your plan and do the work.
- Document your achievements and demonstrate your expertise in the workplace and beyond.

Determine What to Learn

When was the last time you inventoried your portable, marketable skills? Over in the training department of your organization, people routinely do needs assessments to determine what training is needed by various groups of employees. You can do a personal training needs assessment. Choose a time—in January, at the beginning of your organization's fiscal year, on your birthday, on your service anniversary, or today. Then, objectively evaluate your skills in two areas: life skills and job skills.

The Life Skills

It's no surprise that the little books of life's instructions, written by a father for his son who was going off to college, were best-sellers. In trying times—like the freshman year of college or in today's chaotic workplaces—we long for rules, guidelines, and instructions to make sense of the changes we're going through. Taking charge of your own career is about writing your own career life instruction manual. Whether you start when you're eighteen or forty-three, you can identify the skills it takes to make the move toward mastery. In the process, you'll win the bonus prize—an insurance policy on your career.

If you took ten minutes right now to make a list of life skills, what would be on your list? What skills are so general that they spell success in every career?

Here's a list to get you started thinking. Rate yourself on these skills, using a scale of one to ten. (One means, "I'm a complete novice." Ten means, "I've mastered this.") What other skills would you add to the list?

Life Skill	**1**	**2**	**3**	**4**	**5**	**6**	**7**	**8**	**9**	**10**
Learning how to learn										
Managing time										
Prioritizing										

Life Skill	1	2	3	4	5	6	7	8	9	10
Communicating										
Finding information/ resources										
Listening										
Planning										
Resolving conflicts										
Using today's tools (computers, etc.)										
Coaching										
Team building										
Influencing										
Negotiating										
Making presentations										
Budgeting										
Allocating resources										
Networking										
Appreciating differences										
Measuring results										
Celebrating successes										

As you look at how you rated yourself, can you see skills you need to improve? Before you begin to draft your plan for improvement, assess how you're doing on another set of skills, ones that are specific to your job.

Your Job Skills

In addition to the life skills used in almost any job, there are job-specific skills. Most people can recite their job descriptions easily enough, but haven't taken the next step, translating those responsibilities into specific skills to be mastered or continually updated.

If your job description says, "Produce monthly newsletter," what skills do you need to make that publication an organizational or even an industry standout, something you'd be proud to show at your next job interview?

If your job description says, "Manage cost analysis function," what must you know how to do? Research the competition? Establish pricing structures? Predict the long-term impact of political trends on your market?

Nancy is the new advertising director at an insurance company headquarters. She has a solid background in writing, but she's never run an ad department before. Many aspects of her job are completely new to her. "Frankly, I didn't have a clue about some of my responsibilities," she confesses. After floundering around for a few months, she decided to translate her job description into specific skills. Here's what she came up with.

Job Description	Skill Gap
Plans and coordinates ad campaigns	Budgeting for campaigns ($1 million budget)
	Buying graphic design/layout
	Making decisions about in-house vs. outside purchase of materials
	Tracking regulatory and legal constraints
	Buying radio and TV time
	Researching audiences
	Setting criteria for agency selection
	Understanding printing terminology
	Supervising print production
	Selecting which trade press to advertise in

Job Description	Skill Gap
Develops point of sale materials, sales solicitation materials, and direct mail campaigns	Knowing state of the art in of point-of-sale materials, sales solicitation materials, and direct mail campaigns
Coordinates staff of artist/designer, copywriter, support staff	Evaluating design
	Editing the work of others

After she defined the skills she needed, Nancy created her long-term improvement plan. ''Knowing I had a plan helped me feel less stressed. As I figured out the big picture, I got better at choosing short-term opportunities to learn. I could see that eventually I'd get around to focusing on all my skill gaps.'' She got off to a fast start. In a three-month period, she took an in-house training course on the insurance business. She found a mentor to advise her on the ins and outs of purchasing media time. She began her master's degree program in communication management. She attended a meeting of her professional association on print production.

Nancy identified the job skills she needed and went after them, using a variety of learning options. As her skills improved, so did her confidence about performing well in her current job. She also feels good about being able to present herself as a well-qualified candidate for other jobs, if a rumored downsizing hits her department.

Overcome Your Roadblocks

When you identify your skill gaps, you may feel exhilarated about being one step closer to mastering your job and creating career security. On the other hand, you may feel overwhelmed. Unless you understand your roadblocks to learning, you will be unwilling—perhaps even unable—to begin to create your action plan.

Take a pen and jot down any obstacles that come up when you think of learning. Put your feelings of resistance into words. Getting clear about what stands in your way will help you move through the anguish of analyzing your deficiencies and on to the action of filling your gaps.

The roadblocks that hold people back fall into three categories: time and money, energy, and negative memories of previous educational experiences.

Time and Money: John's concerns are the ever-present ones—time and money. "I don't have the hours or the bucks to go for more education and training," he groans. "I've got my kids' education to save for. And besides, whatever happened to leisure time?"

Be creative about finding the time and money to learn for mastery. There's something to fit everyone's schedule and pocketbook.

Can you find some wasted time that you could reclaim for your fireproofing program? Commuting time? TV time? Lunchtime? An hour before the rest of the household wakes up or an hour after they go to bed? The value you create in terms of future career advancement, salary increases, and overall career protection will make rearranging your schedule to work on closing your skills gaps worth the trouble.

Take advantage of tuition reimbursement programs offered by your employer. Remarkably, one study found that only 10 percent of all eligible employees use these programs. Apply for grants or scholarships from professional associations or other institutions. One foundation, part of an association for meeting planners, for example, awards $500 to a deserving member to help pay some costs incurred in earning industry certification.

Energy: Hernando's got his nose to the grindstone, and it's wearing him down. "I'm just trying to use every shortcut in the book to meet my deadline," he says. "And after that, there'll be another deadline. I haven't got the energy to think about learning. I've got to get the job done."

If your life is a video game in which the better you get at whizzing around the curves, the faster the road comes at you, then it's time to pull over and look at a map. The tension created by working excessive overtime with constant pressure may get the job done in the short run, but it isn't good for you or for your organization over the long haul. "Take time to sharpen the saw," says Stephen Covey, in his best-selling book, *The Seven Habits of Highly Effective People.* Take time to enhance the greatest asset you have—yourself. Develop a lifestyle that observes the natural cycle of learning and renewal.

Negative Memories: Lila's unhappy memories of school make her avoid learning situations. "I'm not somebody who did well in school," she says. "I hated sitting there listening to some prof drone on and on. I always clutched during tests. I hope to avoid school the rest of my life. Besides, my boss will tell me if there's a course she wants me to take."

It's true. Not everyone remembers the classroom with pleasure. Many people's memories focus on boredom, embarrassment, and failure. If that describes your experience, look around for innovative, nontraditional programs that will fit your learning style. Build on your strengths. Researchers have identified a variety of learning styles. You could work with a career counselor to design a program that matches your interests and your preferred modes of receiving and mastering information. Think beyond the traditional classes you knew in high school or college. You'll find something just right for you on our list of 101 learning opportunities, which begins on page 150.

Passively waiting around for your boss to tell you what to learn isn't smart if you want to fireproof your career. Your organization is no longer in charge of developing your skills or drafting your career mastery plan. You are.

Discover How and Where to Learn

To expand your thinking about all of the possible ways you might tackle your knowledge gaps, here's a list of 101 learning opportunities. Browse through the list. Experiment with nontraditional settings, unusual formats, and new technologies. No matter what your roadblock or reservation, you're sure to find options that will fit your needs.

101 Learning Opportunities

1. Apprenticeships: Paid or unpaid apprenticeships let you learn from a master.

> After Art finished his law degree, he said, "It will be fine with me if I never see the inside of another classroom." Then he took a communication and conflict resolution course. "That course dramatically improved my relationship with my wife. I told the instructor I'd like to take it about twenty times, just to keep reminding myself of the skills." Art's instructor had a better idea. "He suggested I enroll in the two-year mastery course, which allowed me to be an apprentice teacher so that I could learn how to teach the course," says Art. "Now that I've graduated, I teach the class twice a year. The skills not only enrich my homelife, I know they help me resolve conflicts with my partners at work, too."

2. Audiotape or Videotape Yourself: See yourself in action and assess yourself on skills like speaking, negotiating, managing meetings, or interacting with customers.

3. Audiotapes: Order tapes from mail-order suppliers or bookstores, or check them out at the library.

4. Auditing: If you don't care about accumulating credits for a degree, then you can audit a class at a college or university. Auditing a class usually costs less than being enrolled for credit.

5. Award-winning programs: Review award-winning projects. For example, members of the International Association of Business Communicators can borrow award-winning case studies and work plans to study. They are available through the organization's Communication Bank. If your organization

is part of the quality movement, you can study the Tota
ity Management programs of companies that have wo
Deming Award or the Baldrige Award.

*6. **Benchmarking:*** Determine the leader in a field and make that person or organization your standard.

*7. **Board Service:*** Serve on the board of directors of an organization to strengthen a variety of management skills and to learn from the expertise of other board members.

*8. **Books, How-to:*** Find practical help on an incredible number of topics at bookstores or at the library. For mail-order career books, see *The Whole Work Catalog* from The New Careers Center, Inc., 1515 Twenty-third Street, P.O. Box 339-CT, Boulder, CO 80306, or *The Career Book Catalog* from Impact Publications, 9104 N. Manassas Drive, Manasses Park, VA 22111; 703/361-7300.

*9. **Books, Textbooks.*** If you never took a course on marketing for example, but need to learn the skills, go to a college bookstore and buy a text.

*10. **Camps for Adults:*** Educational vacations are growing in popularity. For instance, Cornell's Adult University Education Vacations program offers weekend seminars, week-long domestic study tours, and study tours abroad on topics ranging from Comedy Acting to Navigating Wall Street: A Guide to Securities Analysis and Portfolio Management.

*11. **Certification Programs:*** These programs are usually offered through associations.

Here's what the National Speakers Association requires members to do to receive its coveted Certified Speaking Profession (CSP) designation.

- Be a member for thirty-six continuous months.
- Serve a minimum of 100 different clients in a five-year period.
- Give a minimum of 250 fee-paid presentations in that five-year period.
- Receive a minimum of $50,000 for each of the five years in speaking fees.

- Submit twenty testimonial letters from clients.
- Acquire thirty-two credits of professional education at NSA national conventions, workshops, conferences, or chapter membership.

12. Churches or Religious Organizations: The Jewish Vocational Service in suburban Cleveland provides workshops on job hunting, for example.

13. Civic and Community Groups: These programs, perhaps run through your city's economic development office, cover topics such as block grants, zoning laws, or environmental awareness.

14. Clinics: A real estate agent, who coaches kids' soccer teams, took a four-day advanced clinic on coaching skills.

15. Coaching: Coaching works best in one-on-one or in small group sessions. In this intensive learning environment, you can improve your skills quickly. Lawyers, for instance, have had great success improving their stage presence and dramatic abilities with help from a director at Arena Stage in Washington, D.C.

16. Colloquia: Set up an exchange or dialogue with others in your field. Myra brought together organizational communication and human resources professionals from the U.S. and Canada for quarterly informal discussions that led to new insights about employee communication in organizations.

17. Community Classes: Parks and recreation departments offer more than swimming lessons. In an evening program, Jim learned software skills that helped him transfer smoothly to a new department when his function was outsourced.

18. Community Colleges, Junior Colleges, Trade Schools: Bone up on math or business writing. Begin or continue your work toward a degree or diploma.

19. Community Leadership Programs: Often sponsored by chambers of commerce, these programs provide leadership training, seminars on business topics, mentoring, and activities designed to increase awareness of diversity and community needs.

20. Computer-Assisted Learning: Thousands of programs are available to help you learn, using your computer. Want to apply for a government job? There's a software program that teaches you how to fill out a 171, the government job application form.

21. Conferences and Conventions: At local, regional, and national events, you'll be able to choose from many sessions, as well as hear keynote speakers talk about trends and industry-specific topics.

22. Consultants: Hire one to teach you what you need to know. Martin edits the company newsletter. Because he thought it could be more readable, he found a consultant to assess the readability of the publication and to provide suggestions on improving it.

23. Correspondence Courses: Learn in the comfort of your home or the convenience of your office. Mail in your assignments and get college credit or feedback from experts.

24. Counseling: For insight into yourself or for making a career change, check out counseling services at your local mental health clinic, university, or one of the many private career counseling services.

25. Courses in Stores: A craft store might offer woodworking courses; a florist might teach Japanese flower arranging and how to care for bonsai, for example.

26. Critiques: Criticism services from professional associations, writers' conferences, etc., can help you improve skills. Some awards programs also include critiques of projects you submit. That's a good way to get feedback on your projects from experts in the field.

27. Cross Company Visits: Call your counterpart at another company and ask to visit to see how someone else gets the job done. A college administrator and his task force visited three other community colleges before making recommendations on how to provide more support services for students who speak English as a second language.

28. Direct Sales and Franchise Support: These companies teach their people how to run a business. They also provide motivational seminars and supply product information.

29. Distance Learning: Take college course work through your computer.

> "My degree will be my career insurance policy," confides Jeanette, who manages a recreation program for employees at a large corporation. "The vice president who sponsors my program will retire in three years. I have no idea whether his replacement will find these corporate sports and leisure time programs worth funding. So, I decided to complete my degree in something marketable: business management and communications. In the little town in Upstate New York where I work, there aren't any colleges, so, I enrolled in the distance learning program at the Rochester Institute of Technology." Jeanette watches the videotaped lectures on her VCR, completes her assignments, takes tests on her computer, and communicates with other students and professors via electronic mail. She also can call her professors on an 800 number. "It's perfect for me. I never leave home. And I like the independence and flexibility," she says.

30. 800 Numbers: Dial for free and find out where to hold a retreat for your board of directors or get help with a computer software program. A directory of 800 numbers is available at the library.

31. Expert Session: Every year, eight dentists, who graduated together, hire a cutting edge speaker to teach them for two days at a resort location. Responsibility for choosing the expert for their reunion rotates among the members, who all chip in to pay his or her fee.

32. Extension Divisions of Universities: You can take workshops on everything from working at home to improving your resumé. You can attend special conferences and can even request special programs that target your unique interest.

33. Feedback from a Trusted Observer: Ask someone to watch your performance and give you tips on improving it.

34. Field Trips: Go to see someone's catfish farm, printing plant, or in-house video department. Call first to ask the owner or director for a guided tour.

35. Games: Whoever said learning had to be dull? Chambers of Commerce, nationwide, offer a simulation computer game that allows you to practice communication skills by "attending" a party at the U.S. Embassy in Paris.

36. Government: The Small Business Administration conducts monthly workshops on how to start a business. Other government agencies provide training, too. The Government Printing Office in Washington, D.C., offers brochures on hundreds of topics.

37. Graduate School Programs: Shop around for the best program for you. Many master's programs offer schedules and content that cater to adult learners. You'll "see other companies" through case studies, experiment with new skills in a risk-free environment, network with other students and professors, get acquainted with resources and experts in your field, and show your company you have initiative and ambition. One nontraditional program is offered by The Fielding Institute in Santa Barbara, California. It's billed as "a graduate school for midlife, mid-career adults." The institute's approach includes "contract-based learning, student initiative and faculty response, mentored study, competence-based assessment, flexible learning settings, and technology-based networking," designed to develop each student into a scholar-practitioner. Its programs include clinical psychology and human and organization development.

38. Hands-On: Some people learn best by leaping in and fiddling around.

Doug is a senior analyst doing project management with a major long-distance company. "I've had two supervisors who handed me a program book with one hand and an assignment with the other. They never even checked up on me; they just wanted the job done. That was a powerful incentive to learn. I just tinkered around until I had it,'' he says.

He has an undergraduate degree in Greek and Hebrew. With a knack for learning languages, he's now fluent in Spanish and French. He's taking Russian at work using his company's individual learning center. Students meet in a classroom setting, then use tapes and books in carrels.

Doug's finishing up his master's in media communication and says he summarizes material to be learned on three-by-five-inch cards, covers them with plastic wrap, and goes jogging. By the time he's through, he's memorized one card front and back. ''Memorizing while exercising seems to go twice as fast as memorizing at my desk,'' he says.

39. Hobbies: Learn while you pursue a hobby. Robert and Evelyn, for example, collect antiques. They are becoming experts on Early American furniture. They learn from dealers and other collectors, as well as from more traditional resources, like books. They plan to open an antique store when Robert retires. Another example is Rebecca, who makes African-American dolls dressed in African costumes to sell at fairs and jazz festivals. She is becoming an expert in both textiles and clothing. Eventually, she intends to start her own gift shop.

40. Home Study Courses. School in a box can be delivered to your door. Unlike correspondence courses, you won't get a grade or send assignments to a teacher for feedback, but you will have well-organized materials to study.

41. Imported-to-Site Training: Find a dozen or more people at work who need training in some area not covered by in-house training programs. Ask the training department to bring a program in-house or pool funds from various departments to pay for the class.

42. Industry Meetings: Learn more about your industry at a meeting like those offered by the Golf Course Superintendents Association for people who manage golf courses.

43. In-House Training: Your company's training department probably offers many courses, from time management to seminars on the insurance industry. If it doesn't offer what you need, ask for it and encourage the department to add the course to its curriculum.

44. Inside Resources: Ask people in other departments to teach you what they do.

> Nancy became advertising director without much knowledge of print production. She went to her in-house print shop and asked the supervisor for help. "Will you give me a short course in printing and an introduction to the terminology and processes?" she asked. She spent about four hours over a month's time and learned the lingo and what to provide to the printers so that the process runs most efficiently. The printing supervisor said, "Thanks for making us take the time to educate you. You've saved us a lot of time and trouble in the long run, and I have a much better idea of what I need to do to produce the kind of quality printed pieces your department needs."

45. Intensive Off-Site Programs: Programs like those offered at the Center for Creative Leadership in Greensboro, North Carolina, focus on broadening your educational background or providing renewal.

46. Interactive Learning Networks: Dial up specialized bulletin boards on your computer. Dialogue and share with others, post questions, and exchange resources.

47. Internships: Some internships are paid; others are not. They're a good way to make job transitions or to get work experience before you're hired. Martha, returning to work after being a stay-at-home mom, completed a master's degree and then found an internship at the magazine edited by of one of her professors. This internship later led to freelance writing assignments with the magazine.

48. Interview an Expert: Ask a guru to be a resource. Sherri was writing a book on team-building. At a professional meeting, she met a retired author and asked to interview him about the writing and publishing process.

49. Jobs: Take a part-time job and learn new skills, such as inventory control, purchasing, or troubleshooting.

50. Journal Writing: Keep a journal to track your progress in developing a new idea or to monitor and evaluate your progress in handling conflict, for example.

51. Judging Awards Programs: This activity gives you a chance to take a look at the best work in your field. Ben judged ad campaigns for the annual Ad Club competition. Sheila evaluated video employee orientation programs for her professional association. Henri critiqued graduate architectural students' projects.

52. Learning from Experience: David chaired a quality team. He said he took weekly lessons on how to implement quality processes from the best school, The School of Hard Knocks.

53. Lecture Series. Look to unlikely sources for lectures on practically everything. Don got information on new technologies at a museum slide show. Rachel prepared for a business trip to Japan by attending a lecture sponsored by a travel agent.

54. Libraries: Libraries are great places to learn and great places to learn how to learn. They might offer minicourses in using databases or helping your child succeed in school.

55. Loaned Executive Programs: Your company might loan you to the United Way or the school board for a special assignment that could provide rich opportunities to learn new skills and that would help you find new approaches to solve the problems your company faces.

56. Magazines and Professional Journals: These publications will keep you up to date, alert you to trends and developments, and teach you about new career areas.

57. Manufacturers' or Dealers' Training Classes: These classes are sometimes offered when you buy products or specialized equipment.

58. Mentors: Develop a long-term relationship with someone who can provide guidance and advice and help steer you toward your career goals.

59. Military Service: Though the military is cutting back, you still may be able to join the reserves or National Guard and take advantage of many skill-building programs and courses and on-the-job training.

60. Museums: With earphones to help you take a guided tour, you can learn a lot by just wandering around a museum or aquarium. These cultural organizations also often offer courses, tours, and hands-on, skill-building classes.

61. Networking: Life is an information interview. The people you meet, anywhere, anytime, can provide vital information.

> Bob, who owns a gourmet food business, always talks to his seat mates on airplanes. Once, he found himself sitting next to the sales representative for a box company. The sales rep connected Bob with one of the box company's designers. She came up with a heart-shaped design for Bob's new gourmet jelly gift box.

62. Newspapers: Look for trends, how-to articles, experts quoted, financial advice, how other people do their jobs, ads for learning opportunities of many kinds.

63. Nonprofit Organizations: The Red Cross may offer information on crisis management planning; youth organizations often provide leadership training.

64. On-the-Job Training from Supervisors or Peers: This is the most common kind of training in the U.S. Don't discount its effectiveness, just because it may happen casually and spontaneously.

65. Open Universities: These short, inexpensive, noncredit programs are offered in most larger cities and college towns.

> Donna, director of finance for a pharmaceutical company, took courses on starting a business, catering, and cooking. She hopes, eventually, to switch careers and open a restaurant. Meanwhile, she's soaking up knowledge.

66. Outdoor Programs: Outward Bound is the most famous, but other smaller programs may be available in your city. They teach skills in such areas as risk-taking, confidence-building, communication, and teamwork.

67. Peer Groups: People with similar jobs can learn from each other.

> Paul, a consultant, facilitates a group of thirteen CEOs who get together monthly to discuss issues and help each other solve problems. Even if you're not a CEO, you could put together such a group and hire a consultant to run it or lead it yourself.

68. Performance Tryouts: Watch then do, under the eye of someone who has the skill. Connie, who is new to the field, watched Leroy work with children in an art therapy class. Then he observed her doing the same activity and gave her feedback on her performance.

69. Phone Training: A paper company provides expert help on computer and computing problems for a fee—even on weekends—after you enroll in its support plan. (Call 800/PC-FIX-IT for information.)

70. Professional Associations: These organizations provide a wealth of learning opportunities. If you are changing careers, seek out the association that serves the field you want to move into. Professional development possibilities include workshops, monthly programs, networking opportunities, annual conferences, career information and job banks, the association's magazine or newsletter, audiotapes, and many other ways to learn new skills or improve your performance. To find the association in your field or a field you would like to move into, consult the Encyclopedia of Associations at your library.

71. Reference Desk at the Library: For quick, accurate information on practically anything, call or visit your public library. Many systems now have a special reference line you can call from your home or office.

72. Renewal Programs: These programs help you get in touch with yourself and set personal goals. They may also help you fill in the gaps in your education, introducing engineers to art history, for example.

73. Role Playing: Practice behaviors and learn new ways of reacting by role playing. Ask someone if you can watch him talk to a customer, then try it out. Let the expert be the account representative, while you play the customer. Then reverse roles and discuss what happened.

74. Sales Literature: From step-by-step instructions to ideas for application of services or products, consult the sales materials.

75. Self-assessment: Tests from the career counseling center at a college, assessments from a professional association, or quizzes from newspapers, magazines, and books can help you learn about yourself and determine your skill level or gaps.

"After I graduated from college twelve years ago, I landed a job as a dietician at a large children's hospital," says Ron. "I received good performance ratings and attended conventions to keep up in my field. But I didn't have any objective way to measure my skill level, especially in light of all the advancements in the last decade. Then my professional group, the American Dietetic Association, announced self-assessment modules. I filled out the assessment, sent it in, and the scores came back to me, not my employer. It was all very confidential. It helped me set priorities for my continuing education."

76. Shadowing: Follow a skilled person as he or she completes a project.

77. Seminar Companies' Offerings: Get on the mailing list of a variety of companies or check out upcoming seminars through your company's training department.

78. Special Assignments: Take on a temporary assignment or work on a special task force. Bell Atlantic trained people from marketing and operator services to teach a career management seminar three days a month. Many of those teachers eventually moved into full-time training.

79. Special Interest Groups: Toastmasters offers people opportunities to improve their public speaking skills. An investment group provides a variety of learning experiences for members who own rental property—everything from tax tips to where to buy the cheapest paint.

80. Sponsored Events: The owner of a marketing company invites customers and potential customers to her Meeting of the Minds events. They learn from each other as well as from her guest speakers.

81. Study Groups: From book clubs run by book stores to investment clubs that teach you how to manage your money, study groups can focus your learning on a particular area.

82. Study Tours: People to People International offers trips to Russia, the Czech Republic, and Poland, for example. As globalization continues, cross-cultural awareness and communication skills will continue to be in demand. Also, you can go on an environmental awareness trip sponsored by a group whose goal is to clean up our rivers.

83. Summer Programs: The Sales and Marketing Executives International has teamed up with Syracuse University's Graduate School of Sales Management and Marketing to offer a two-year program that meets for two intensive weeks of study each summer.

84. Supervising College Interns: Want supervisory experience, but have no subordinates? Take on a college intern.

85. Suppliers and Vendors: You can learn a lot from these folks, and they're usually willing to teach you to encourage you to do business with them.

> Bryan, who owns an office supply business, invited his major suppliers to an appreciation lunch. To drive home the point that, "If we grow, you grow," he asked, "Do you know of other companies that we should be doing business with?" He invited them to make the contact. "Otherwise," he points out, "It's a cold call." As well as customer leads, he got excellent marketing ideas from his suppliers and referrals to other suppliers who could fill some special needs.

86. Support Groups: From groups you create to ones offered by various organizations, you can learn a variety of skills, such as how to manage time, achieve balance in your life, and take time to celebrate your achievements.

87. Simulations: To test out a crisis-management plan or your emergency response capabilities, try a simulation.

88. Teaching: "If you become a teacher, by your students you'll be taught," goes the lyric from the musical, *The King and I.* Federal Express uses managers as teachers in its "university." They return to their jobs after their professorships are over with a deeper understanding of their fields. George Washington University in Washington, D.C., offers a program called Teaching as a Second Career.

89. Templates: For newsletter or brochure design, templates or fill-in-the-blank guides are available. They can act as models for do-it-yourself design projects.

90. Television: Sign up for classes at home or look into bringing courses to your workplace through universities or from other sources, via videoteleconferencing.

91. Total Immersion: These programs offer a quick way to learn a language or understand a culture. On vacation, Lynda lived with a Mexican family for three weeks to improve her chances at landing a job in the international division of her company.

92. Trade Shows and Expositions: The International Franchise Association, for instance, offers seminars, speakers, demonstrations, and product literature at its annual trade show.

93. Tutors: Pay someone to help you bone up or speed-learn new material. Larry hired a language tutor. Madge contracted with an expert to help her get up to speed quickly on her new software.

94. Understudy: Tell your boss, ''You give a lot of speeches. I want to be ready to take over if you are called out of town.'' Then prepare as if you would be giving the presentation or conducting the meeting.

95. Users' Manuals and Documentation: As these things become more and more user friendly, they can be your guides, helping you learn about technical fields and equipment.

96. Users' Meetings: Customers get together to share ideas and tips and give feedback to manufacturers. Long a staple in the computer industry, these meetings could be used by any organization wanting information from customers.

97. Vacation Programs: Have fun and learn, too. The Smithsonian Institution will sign you up for an archaeological dig, for example.

98. Videotapes from Mail-Order Suppliers, Bookstores, or Libraries: A workshop for aspiring novelists is provided through videos plus a workbook and desktop manual. Thousands of topics are now available, from landscape design to how to restore old cars.

99. Volunteering: Another learning-by-doing option, volunteering gives you all kinds of useful skills. People who work for Habitat for Humanity, for example, learn home repair skills.

100. Weekend Programs: Look for these programs from a variety of universities, colleges, and other organizations.

> On the outside, Cheryl appeared to be a very successful computer sales and marketing executive, enthusiastically building a small, new company to $40 million in revenues. But, inside, she was bored. "My job lacked meaning," she says. She enrolled in a master of arts degree program at the University of Santa Monica. Once a month, she flies from her home in Washington, D.C., for her weekend class with 250 other professional people. She likes the intensity. "Don't sell out," she advises, "and enroll in a convenient program you don't like. Life's too short to go through hours of torture just to get a degree. People are always amazed that I'm willing to go to California to school, but it makes perfect sense to me. That's where they have the program and faculty I want."

101. Women's Centers: The Women's Center of Northern Virginia has a program called I CAN. These letters stand for the Information and Career Advisory Network. The network is made up of 630 advisors who are committed to providing information interviews about specific professions. They work with women—and men—who are job hunting or changing careers. With workshops, financial and career counseling, volunteer and leadership opportunities, and myriad other kinds of support, women's centers offer all-round self-development.

Draft Your Plan and Do the Work

After you have assessed your skill gaps and determined learning options, draft your plan. Writing down your goals is essential. Set deadlines. Be specific. Look at the short term and the long term.

Here are the steps—and what one determined learner did to move toward mastery.

- Plan backward. Begin with your long-term goals.
  Sylvia wanted to expand from her base in corporate communications into marketing.
- Break your goal down into logical steps.
  She decided to stop by a university bookstore and buy a basic marketing textbook to get a good overview of the field and to be sure she understood what knowledge and skills she would need to acquire.
- Then list weekly activities.
  She divided the number of chapters in the book by twenty-one days to give herself daily deadlines and entered her reading into her daily planning book. Sylvia finished reading the text and taking notes on it in three weeks.
- List activities that you can do now.
  Sylvia received a meeting announcement from the local chapter of the American Marketing Association. She decided to attend a meeting and asked about membership. Since her antenna was up, lots of information about marketing communications began to appear.
- Check your short-term activities to be sure they put you in position to achieve the long-term goal.
  Sylvia had her sights set on a job in marketing. It took some discipline to plow through the marketing book on her own, but she kept remembering that getting this overview and getting familiar with the jargon was a good move.
- Tell someone else your goal and set a time (after your deadline) to report on your progress to that person.
  Sylvia called Mark, who works in marketing communications for another company and told him what she was doing. She asked if he would meet her for lunch after she had read the text so that she could discuss her next project with him.
- Be on the lookout for other training opportunities.
  Sylvia kept a file labeled Training for Me. In this file, she put book reviews, names of people, flyers about workshops,

and an article from the business section of her local paper on area universities with master's degree programs in marketing.

Your plan is a living document. Check it at regular intervals and add to it as you gain information.

Follow-through is everything. Frank, a consultant, says he's quit providing clients with strategic planning sessions. He now calls them "strategic intending" sessions. And yet, even intending isn't enough. You must take action.

It doesn't make sense to join a professional association, for example, and then not attend meetings, yet that happens all the time. Karl thought, "I don't want to go to the meeting this month. It's on media relations and I don't do media relations in my job." Too bad. He should think beyond his current job and learn skills for his next job.

Check your educational plan every week, and schedule activities on your calendar. Putting your plan into action is the only way to develop your skills. It may seem slow. Each tiny piece of information may seem insignificant by itself. But over the long haul, you will be amassing an amazing amount of expertise.

In a midwestern city, massive layoffs in the aerospace industry were announced in the newspaper. A Small Business Administration official fielded phone calls from the soon-to-be-laid-off workers. He called these conversations "painful." The workers felt totally unprepared, he said, and desperate. The workers were "terribly naive" about starting their own businesses. The skills they had developed in the aerospace industry often were too specialized to transfer easily to other careers or entrepreneurial ventures.

These workers learned too late that they should have been acquiring new skills and preparing for other careers before they were faced with pink slips.

Don't let that happen to you.

Document Your Achievements and Demonstrate Your Expertise

Conrad, who had just been laid off, was sitting in an outplacement class, paid for by his previous employer, working on his resumé. He was trying to remember when he took those computer courses and exactly what they covered. He knew that getting a job might hinge on his being able to verify that he had these classes, but he can't quite remember.

Keep track of your learning activities. Your documentation will not only make sure you have accurate data to put on a resumé, it also will get you motivated as you learn.

Create a learning log to document your expertise. A three-ring notebook will do, or you can keep information on your computer. (If you do keep your log on your computer at work, just be sure to copy it and take it home or print it off, periodically. Sometimes, when people lose their jobs, they immediately lose access to their workplace computers.) In this log, write down learning projects, formal or informal, self-directed or degree-oriented, work-related, or personal.

You will be able to use the information you log in about your learning achievements in your current job, too. Before your next performance evaluation, write a memo to your boss, telling what skills you have developed since your last review.

In your Learning Log, write down

- The date
- The name of the book you read or course you attended or audiotape you listened to or activity you pursued
- The source (so, if necessary, you can find it again)
- The specific knowledge or skill gap this activity applies to
- Any other information you might need later to verify your acquisition of this knowledge
- Ideas for other topics to learn about

Nancy, whose list of skill gaps appears on page 146, made these entries in her log as she learned about print production.

Date	Activity	Source	Skill Gap
9/13	Met with Alvin Day, supervisor, print shop	In-house print shop two-hour, one-on-one session	Print production processes, terminology
10/28	Speaker, Tom Allen, Allen Printing, 555–7110	IABC meeting speaker	Print production

Notice that Nancy jotted down Tom Allen's phone number so that if she has a question, she can call him. She is collecting the names of other local experts to put in her log.

To build your reputation as an expert, find ways to demonstrate your expertise in your workplace and beyond. The best way to solidify a new skill is to find a way to use it immediately.

You can demonstrate and share your expertise by volunteering, writing, speaking, mentoring, networking, consulting, and teaching. Become known as someone who gives information away.

Think of it this way: As you begin your learning program, you can add to your expertise, move toward mastery, and accelerate your progress toward becoming an expert in your field. If you pursue all of these steps, you will have begun to fireproof your career through learning for mastery.

Chapter 9

Lean Out of Specialization

At a large firm going through its first layoffs in forty-three years, this note appeared on the employee bulletin board.

EFFECTIVE IMMEDIATELY
Due to budget cuts,
the light at the end of the tunnel has been turned off.

It used to be that the light shone brightly and all you had to do was settle into a career track, chug along straight ahead, and the reward would be there waiting for you at the end of the tunnel.

Encouragement to think of ourselves as on track and headed toward a specific job title starts early. Adults ask, "What do you want to be when you grow up?" Kids are expected to come up with a good answer. On down the line, the big question is, "What are you majoring in?" Again, we make a choice. It used to be that you'd stick with that choice and a particular company for thirty-five or forty years, and move up, as you updated and improved the same set of basic skills.

In today's workplace that kind of career tracking is gone. Flexibility now tops the list of qualities you need to ensure your continued employability in the constant upheavals that rock our economy and impact our organizations. Recent studies show that most people will have around thirteen distinctly different job titles in their careers. What job titles will you hold throughout your working life? Rather than putting all of your energy into safeguarding your current job, something that may not be within your control, use the strategies in this chapter to help you increase your overall options for employment.

A close friend described to us a conversation she had with her husband, who was celebrating his fiftieth birthday. In a quiet moment, before the party started, she put her arms around him and said, "I'm so proud of you—you really turned out well." He pulled away, looked surprised and a little indignant, and said, "I can't believe you're saying that. I'm not done! I'm still turning out!"

Your ability to continue to turn out—to lean, leap, bridge, transfer, slide, or glide into new or adjacent career areas—will mean the difference between career stagnation and career security in the turbulent times ahead as organizations and entire industries continue to reconfigure themselves. Plan now which career tracks you could switch to if your job, your department, your organization, or your industry is disappearing, even as you read this chapter.

Learn to shape, reshape, and add to the special collection of knowledge, skills, experiences, abilities to learn, and personal qualities that you bring to your job as you make many job changes, some voluntary, some involuntary. Take charge, manage your career. This radical shift in the way you think about your work is not for the weary or the weak of heart. Ethan, who was downsized out of his job near the end of his long and successful career, was weighing the pros and cons of finding a new job versus retiring. Frustrated, he said, "I've had it! I'm not going to look for a job. I've been through too many paradigm shifts and my gears are stripped."

Ethan was worn out because he had spent the last decade trying stave off change. The successful job-holder of the future will take a positive, proactive approach. The challenge is to keep the following realities and questions in mind, as you turn up options for future career moves.

- FACT: The old career paths in most organizations no longer exist. Many of the middle management and administrative tracks are derailing with layoffs or shunting plateaued employees onto a siding. The way to the top is more crowded than ever before, as you and your peers compete with each other for jobs in the upper echelons. The simple fact is, there's not room for everybody at the top.
  CHALLENGE: If you're not going up, where *are* you going? Are you willing to look for other avenues of career advancement and new ways to direct your career, even if they mean moving laterally, changing your skill set, swapping salary for satisfaction, or going outside the organization to entrepreneurship?
- FACT: Massive advances in technology and shifts in global power mean thousands of jobs are disappearing. At the same time, thousands of new ones are opening up.
  CHALLENGE: Are you willing to develop your ability to see new areas of growth and invest time and money in learning new skills to stay competitive?
- FACT: Customer service is the key to cornering any market. Organizations want people who can see problems, be flexible, work comfortably with people from diverse backgrounds, move easily from one responsibility to another, and work in a variety of environments to capture customer commitment.
  CHALLENGE: Are you willing to give up the "That's-not-in-my-job-description" mind-set? Are you willing to respond positively to constant change in organizational priorities, structures, and work groups, and to act in a variety of roles and responsibilities?

Pack Up Your Portable Skills

Have you ever burned the roast and ended up making quite a satisfactory meal from salad, veggies, a hearty loaf of bread and apple pie? If your main career burns out, are you simultaneously stirring up several other possible careers that could keep you from going hungry? Rank yourself on this list of the ten most transferable skills. If you decide you excel at certain skills, use this chapter to explore where else you might apply them. If you need to beef up your skills, refer to chapter 8, "Learn for Mastery," to plan how and where you can develop your expertise.

	None	Novice	Adequate	Expert
1. Managing Budgets	______	______	______	______
2. Leading People	______	______	______	______
3. Relating to Customers and other Publics	______	______	______	______
4. Using Leading Edge Technology	______	______	______	______
5. Writing and Editing	______	______	______	______
6. Managing Projects with Deadlines	______	______	______	______
7. Interviewing and Briefing	______	______	______	______
8. Training and Coaching	______	______	______	______

	None	Novice	Adequate	Expert
9. Coordinating and Organizing	______	______	______	______
10. Influencing and Negotiating	______	______	______	______

Going Places: Twenty Savvy Career Moves

An ancient Greek philosopher said, "Consider the little mouse, how sagacious an animal it is which never entrusts its life to one hole only." Developing several career options is the smart thing to do today. Use the following strategies to explore and develop career possibilities you might not have thought of.

Go Up

If climbing up the ladder to top management is still part of your career plan, don't be surprised if you find yourself getting impatient as you wait in line. Up is the least likely option for success in today's lean organizations. At one newly streamlined Fortune 500 company there is only one general manager job for every 5,500 employees.

Dreams of being the boss are hard to give up. It's tough to relinquish the belief that up is better, up is success, up is power, up is more money. But once you start to develop other options, the downside of up is more apparent: mega stress, long hours, and less time for personal and family pursuits.

If you decide you want to go up, be sure to find a mentor, or better yet, several career advisors. Exceed your goals and let people know how you did it. Build your relationships. Make decisions quickly. In this fast-paced world, just putting in time is out. Making visible contributions to the bottom line is the only way to advance. Consider also the value of detouring out to functional posts, such as manufacturing or finance before setting your sights on an upper management job.

The experience will give you new perspectives and in most systems is not viewed as a demotion as it was in years past. Study your industry trends and anticipate what kinds of expertise your organization will require in the future. Increase your ability to learn to ensure your promotability.

Go Out

Explore the option of going outside your organization to competitors or to other companies that can use your set of skills. Continuing to work in the same capacity but for a different firm is one of the smoothest transitions you can make.

Your fireproofing plan will surely include joining a professional association whose members do what you do but in other industries. Get to know your counterparts in other organizations. Exchanging ideas with them not only leads you to information that will help you do your current job better, but also means you'll hear about upcoming job openings before an ad hits the newspapers. Listen for news of job openings because people are moving, being promoted, or taking time off for family reasons. Read industry newsletters and trade journals to look for other companies that need people who do what you do.

> Sales of new computers had dropped by fifty percent in Sue's department. In the recession, the associations she marketed to just didn't have the money for new hardware. People were leaving in droves and Sue felt lucky to land a lateral ten-month assignment as project manager for a traveling exhibit called "The Office of the Future." She liked her her temporary assignment, so she explored other firms that hired trade show managers and had a job lined up when hers was abolished.

Go Back

That's right. Go back to an old career. Go back to a career you've known and loved. Sometimes, in desperation, people think of going back to a former career they disliked. We don't recommend that for obvious reasons. Satisfaction creates success in whatever you do.

Going back may mean exchanging a bigger salary for a slower pace of life or trading some perceived status for a bit more satisfaction. Not a bad deal when the circumstances are right.

> "There are two things I've hated about my career for nineteen years," said Fred, who was taking a career management class for civilians who work at the Department of Navy, "being inside all day and wearing a necktie!" When final word came that, as part of an overall reorganization, his job was being moved to a site 300 miles away, he decided to go back to operating heavy equipment, something he'd done in his early twenties. "Some people hear what I'm doing and approach me as if there's been a death in the family. I tell them I feel like I've just been let out of prison," he said.

> When Jack, a regional sales manager, heard through the grapevine that a merger and downsizing were around the corner, he took the news as an opportunity to leap back to his previous career as a high school teacher. He saw it as a way to spend more time with his two young sons and reduce the stress in his lifestyle. He gave up $13,000 a year in salary but figured the family would save at least half of that in day care costs because he'd be home with his boys a lot more. During summer vacations, he planned to write that book on sales training that he never had time to get to when he was working fifty-five hours a week as a sales manager. His wife's career as a paralegal was secure,

and she was pleased to have Jack spend more time with the children.

Go Sideways

Look for a lateral move within your organization. Why? If your division is being downsized or isn't performing well, it makes sense to sashay sideways. Experience in several different departments or business units may make you a more valued employee down the road. To be considered for an executive position in one health maintenance organization, you must have developed expertise in several facets of the business.

How do you find out where your skills might help others accomplish their mission? Do some inside networking. Get to know people in other departments and divisions. Serve on a task force, read the organizational newsletter, play on the company volleyball team, or work on a committee that has organization-wide membership. Figure out how your skills as an administrator or systems analyst or manager might be useful in other settings within your organization. Increase your visibility. Polish up and promote your transferable skills.

Look especially hard at your internal vendors and customers—the people whom you serve or who serve you in some way, people in adjacent departments or functions. Sometimes, you can glide sideways and even diagonally upward through various adjacencies.

Pat started her career in the human resources department as a compensation specialist, then moved into training. Soon, she was specializing in sales training. Respect for her expertise grew and she was asked to apply for the job of sales manager. From that job, it was a hop, skip, and a jump to director of marketing for a start-up business unit. Now, she's moved again to become product marketing manager for a product that is sold worldwide.

Carol, with fifteen years of experience in one telecommunications firm, says she and her peers have talked about how an announcement of a lateral move that once was greeted with words of consolation, is now cause for celebration. "The probability of promotion is very slim now, so my strategy is to move around. I've gone from technical support to information systems to business research to collections to new product development." Carol had to convince her boss in new product development that she would indeed be happy, even though the move was a demotion in both title and salary. She made the move because she thought it was wise to cross over to an area with more long-term growth possibilities. "Around here, we just have to keep redefining success," says Carol.

Go Over

Jump over the fence and look to suppliers, customers, or vendors for your next career move. The transition is easy because you already know a lot about their needs. You are more likely to be considered an insider than someone who applies for the job off the street. Suppliers and customers have already experienced your competence and character. You can play up how you can be a problem-solver in their environment when you write your resume and cover letter. And you may be invited to skip some steps in the job interview process because you're a known quantity.

As a trainer in the personnel department, Koro was quite familiar with the services that human resources development firms provided to the hospital where he worked. When rumors of budget cuts and outsourcing circulated, he explored how he could switch to the vendor side and find a position with one of the large, well-respected human resources development firms in

Atlanta. He finished the last two courses in his master's degree, cultivated his relationships in those firms, and landed a position before the hospital's first round of cuts was even announced.

Go Narrow

A business consultant had this piece of advice: "The narrower the niche, the fatter the fee." He's on to something. Stories abound of companies that decided to get out of a specific market or product niche and were willing to sell off the business to an employee or group of employees. Or, you might discover an unmet need or an unserved customer.

Lawyers are a dime a dozen, but Jerome, noticing the intense interest in franchising, decided to specialize in helping prospective franchisees narrow their choices and deal with the legalities. His practice is booming.

Go Home

More people than ever before are going home to go to work. Do any of your career skills lend themselves to a home-based business? Join the crowd! By the end of 1993, more than 41.1 million Americans—that's one-third of the workforce—were homeworkers. Of those, 24.3 million were running full-time or part-time businesses from their dens or basements. (Company employees who work at home during normal business hours total 7.6 million and after-hours homeworkers total 9.2 million, says LINK Resources, a research and consulting firm that conducts an annual National Work-at-Home Survey.)

Starting a business at home is easier than ever before. In fact, a new home-based business starts every eleven seconds! One reason for that upsurge is that the technology to operate from home but stay in touch with the world is more available and affordable than ever before. For a few thousand dollars you can have a phone, a fax, a computer, a copier, and overnight mail service that picks up and delivers to your door. Other reasons that make working from home an obvious plus are the low overhead, the convenience, and the ability to be on hand when family needs arise. Many of your most portable skills can be carried out in a business from the home: writing, speaking, teaching, selling, consulting, and all kinds of information-based client services.

> Beverly was told that her job as managing editor of technical publications would be abolished in four months. She used that time to set up her home office in her guest bedroom. Her biggest risk was the small business loan she took to buy computer equipment. She offered technical editing, newsletter writing and editing, and some computer graphics to a wide variety of clients. Networking through home-based business organizations, she developed her own client base, as well as valuable relationships with desktop publishers, who subcontracted work to her when they were overloaded.

Go South

Combine a career option with a lifestyle option, and you may choose to "go south," as one fellow, put it. How could relocation serve to open up new opportunities and reduce your living costs? Could you move to a warmer, slower, less expensive environment? A smaller town? Your hometown? Closer to relatives? What change in lifestyle or environment might ease financial or lifestyle stress or expand your worklife options?

> When Bob and Marie began to discuss the possibility that Bob would soon be laid off from his aerospace job in Seattle, they both agreed an option was to move back home to South Carolina. Marie's skills as a nurse

and masseuse were portable. Bob began to explore sales and management positions with prospective employers in Columbia. The couple was lured by the warmer weather, the slower pace, the lower cost of living, and the idea of being closer to all their relatives. The money they got for their Seattle home allowed them to pay cash for a house in Columbia and eased their financial concerns until Bob found a job as a sales rep for an automotive parts manufacturing company.

Go Inland

New business concepts and trends are said to begin on the coasts and move slowly inland. There also are plenty of innovative ideas in Middle America. If you're scouting for a new business idea, look East or West and take it to the Middle—or vice versa!

When Jill moved to Kansas City from Washington, D.C., several years ago, there was only one thing she missed—great French bread. So, she and her husband began to research how French bakers get that distinctive flaky crust and chewy middle and discovered they'd have to import a special French oven and a French chef. They did just that and opened a French bakery and café.

Sally, a Des Moines, Iowa, banker with a hankering to be an entrepreneur, methodically researched business ideas. She was intrigued by the mail-order steak business that's put beef from Omaha, Nebraska, on tables from Takoma to Tokyo. Then, she discovered the Iowa pork chop and decided to replicate the steak business with "the other white meat." Originally, the company subcontracted everything, but when the company was only two years old, it outgrew its supplier, and Sally and her partner had to buy a meat packing plant. They had planned to sell in five to seven years, but opportunity came knocking when the business was only four years old. Sally is now researching new business ideas and plans another start-up soon.

Go Global

Widen your career horizons with an international assignment. A year or two in the Bangkok or Barcelona office could be an enormous plus for your career as global markets grow and multinational businesses boom. Taking an assignment in Australia, Mexico, or Canada can add to your career security package because, in addition to the new cultures, languages, and business practices you'll learn about, you will surely stand out as a flexible and adaptable person.

Everyone in the company Marcella worked for sensed more lean times ahead. Early retirement packages had been offered twice. The joke around the office was, ''If you take your running shoes home over the weekend, be sure to bring them back on Monday—you'll need them when the weekly reorganization is announced!'' Marcella was fairly confident that if layoffs came, she wouldn't be hit. Of twenty-six field supervisors in operator services, she ranked number one in seniority. But when she was offered an eight-month assignment training operators in New Zealand, she saw it as a way to broaden her career options, in case her department was replaced by improved technology in the next downsizing. Not only would she get international experience, she'd also add stand-up training to her list of portable skills.

Go Temp

The U.S.'s largest employer is a temporary placement firm. Temporary employment is available to nurses, lawyers, accountants, CPAs, doctors, teachers, executives, and many other white-collar professionals. Typically, you sign on project-by-project or client-by-client, or for a specific time period.

Consider registering simultaneously with several agencies in your field. You also might register with a temp firm in a city you're thinking of moving to, so you can try out what it would be like to live there. You could combine temping with starting your own business. A temporary placement can tide you over when you don't have enough work of your own. Think of it as a continuous string of jobs where you have the freedom to stop when you want to for whatever reason—a summer off with the kids, an extended vacation, or an intensive six-week course to improve your credentials. Some obvious considerations are how to plan for your health and life insurance and how you'll handle taxes, since many firms treat you as an independent contractor.

Mary Ann's architectural firm had already let five people go in response to dwindling contracts. She imagined if things didn't improve, she'd be next. When word came that her mother was terminally ill, she decided to move temporarily to San Diego to be with her. She found a renter for her house, signed on with a temporary firm that placed architects in San Diego, put some things in storage, and moved in with her mother. Mary Ann was able to take short assignments and still spend time with her mother and supervise her care. "I wonder if I'll ever take a full-time assignment again. I like the pace of working very intensively, then having time off," she says.

George was three months into his first job as a radiation-oncology staff member, when the small-town hospital where he worked began to lay off people. George, who was young, single, and loved to travel, registered with an agency that specialized in medical temporaries. He requested assignments in three cities: New York, Boston, and Washington. The agency made all the arrangements including travel and housing. Some assignments were for a week or two, some a little longer. In addition to enjoying his time off in the big city, George was gaining valuable experience, creating an outstanding resume, and developing a wide network of professional and personal contacts.

Go Part Time

The rise in part-time employment is another sign of the trend away from the traditional American workday. Four out of five U.S. firms now employ part-time help as a way to keep a lid on costs. You could consider part-time employment as a way to buy time while you look for full-time work. More and more white-collar professionals actively seek part-time positions for other reasons: They want more family or personal time, they see part-time work as a way to try out a new career area, or they want to retire from full-time employment gradually. On the negative side, employers don't usually offer benefits to part-timers. If, however, you can get your benefits through your spouse's organization or a professional association, part-time employment may be a smart career move.

When Ann's twins were born, she took six weeks of maternity leave, then returned to full-time work. The schedule was hectic and stressful, especially when her husband's job took him out of town for several weeks at a time. Soon after the health research company she worked for was bought by a firm in Massachusetts, her vice president announced that all jobs would be moved to the headquarters in Boston. She decided to look for a part-time rather than full-time position so she could spend more time with her three-year-old twins. The job she found allowed her to work at home on her computer for most of her twenty-hour work week. Since she was a night owl, much of that time was between 8 P.M. and midnight. She reasoned that although it was a cut in salary, she improved the quantity and quality of time she spent with her children, saved money by not having to commute, spent less money on professional clothing, and dramatically reduced her day-care costs.

Go Innovate

Noticing their cat watching television, a couple decided to create videos for cats. Short on plot but long on action, the videos feature mice scurrying, fish swimming, birds fluttering, and balls bouncing. Naturally, these videos are marketed to cat lovers and not to their impecunious felines. There are entire catalogs of products for cat people and dog people.

Lots of us have ideas for products or services. Most of us don't do anything about bringing them to market. Often invention is the result of taking an idea and applying it in a new way. When women left the kitchen for the workplace, they quit baking and using baking soda. About that same time, someone decided that baking soda made an effective air freshener in refrigerators. Voila! A new use for an old product. Sometimes, shifting the target market is all that's necessary. First microwave dinners, then microwave dinners for kids. Packaging also lends itself to creativity. MacDonald's Happy Meal is an excellent example.

Inventing is something you can easily do while you're still employed.

Justin is a mechanical engineer for a successful but small firm that will very likely be bought and sold several times as it grows. On weekends and holidays, he moonlights as an inventor. A Vietnam veteran who lost both his legs in combat, he became very interested in wheelchair construction. He is currently working on improvements to the wheels so they can turn more easily on gravel or rocky surfaces.

Go Entrepreneur

"Nothing increases your security like working for yourself," reports one recent escapee from the corporate golden handcuffs. "I'll never be laid off again," she says confidently.

Even if you've never thought of yourself as the entrepreneurial type, try taking a fresh look at this way of recareering. What skills, interests, aptitudes, and relationships do you have that might lead to some sort of more direct relationship with the consumer? Being careful to abide by any "non compete" agreements you have with your current employer, ask yourself, "How could I serve my current customers or clients directly?" Or explore the idea of starting a business using a skill or interest not currently used in your job.

Management announced that the closed circuit TV division of a large electronics firm would be closed down in one year. Angelina, a well-respected and valued employee, was invited to make a lateral move to another unit of the corporation, but the assignment didn't appeal to her. Instead, she went into business with her brother, a retired state policeman. They sold and installed security systems in doorways, elevators, and parking lots. She had always been good with gadgetry and, with her electronics background, she was familiar with the technology. Her brother brought to the business an extensive network of contacts in the community from his work in crime prevention. Together they made an unbeatable combination, as they capitalized on the business world's growing interest in security devices.

Six months before Mike was laid off from his job as the vice president of training for a large pharmaceutical firm, he took two steps that helped him move into entrepreneurship. To create an identity for his new business, he hired a graphic artist who designed business cards, stationary, and a brochure describing Mike's training services. In the evenings, he began to teach a course for graduate students on how to design training. By the time he was officially given the word that his job had been abolished, he had already lined up enough freelance training work to earn one-third of his next year's salary. The network he was building with his students in the evening course turned out to be a gold mine. With a whole semester to develop those relationships and his expert status clearly defined, he landed two large contracts with companies that his students worked for.

Go Franchise

The word *franchise* literally means "to be free." It's one way to own, manage, and direct your own business—within the rules and regulations spelled out in your agreement or contract with the franchisor.

John Naisbitt, author of *Megatrends 2000,* has called franchising "the wave of the future," and for good reason. A new franchise outlet opens somewhere in the U.S. every six and a half minutes. In 1992, franchise businesses accounted for more than $757.8 billion in sales and employed more than 7.2 million people. As with any business or career move, there are pros and cons. The franchisor-franchisee relationship is crucial, and the initial investment can be sizable, so you'll want to research the business carefully and proceed cautiously. No matter what your skills or interests, there's a business to suit you. From food to formal wear, shipping services to security systems, janitorial to sign-making services, there are more than sixty different industries to choose from.

"Where is *our* life?" David and Nancy asked themselves. "We're like ships passing in the night." The kids were grown, and the couple's careers had completely taken over. They both worked many hours of overtime trying to climb their corporate ladders and stay in favor as the rumor mill churned out predictions of downsizing. On New Year's Day, they decided to take three months to research how they could design careers that would allow them to work together. On February 1, Nancy was offered a very good severance package and took it. She spent several months taking courses in small business management and preparing for entrepreneurship.

David found himself hoping he would be laid off, too. Since he had worked longer for his company than Nancy had worked for hers, he thought his offer would be very good, so he tried to hang on. However, by August, he was fed up, wanted to get on with his life, and decided to resign. One month later, David and Nancy opened their business together—a franchised house-cleaning service. Two years later, they've bought another franchise and are very glad they redesigned their lives.

Anita was tired of hassles over declining membership revenues and worried about talk of outsourcing much of the work in the publications department of the association where she worked. She decided to buy a franchise as a route to being her own boss. She attended the International Franchise Show, studied industry trends and franchise profiles, and talked with experts. She was ready to leap when her boss announced that she would have to lay off three of the four people she supervised. Anita suggested that she go instead!

Using her severance pay, vacation pay, and the equity in her house, she bought a quick print shop in a great location. In the second year of operation, her volume tripled and she hired three part-time employees. "I got into this because I realized that I could sell the services that I used to buy!" she says. "I was attracted because I already knew the terminology and what constitutes customer service in the printing industry. I'd been a customer! I've always been interested in the printing business. My first job as a teenager was mimeographing the church programs."

Go Help

Ninety-four million Americans volunteer an average of four hours a week, according to a Gallup survey. Why? As if the obvious benefit of helping to improve the quality of life for others isn't enough, when you help others, you feel more powerful and in charge. You are appreciated, which will probably be a boost if you've been feeling undervalued by your full-time employer. You rub shoulders with active, positive people—pillars of the community and business leaders—who may now become active members of your network. Of course, volunteering is also a way to learn new skills. Volunteering definitely adds to your career security plan on many levels.

Since time and energy are at a premium, choose carefully where to place yourself. The options are endless, so set up criteria that you'll feel good about. Do you want to learn new skills or use skills you already have? Do you want to work with kids or adults? With animals or with people? Alone or in a group? In a program your company sponsors or on your own, without any corporate identification? On the front lines or behind the scenes? In what industry setting (political, medical, environmental, etc.) would you like to volunteer? Take your volunteer job seriously, and it can bring you great satisfaction as well as more career mobility. You can volunteer a few hours a week and use it as a bridge to a new career, or you can volunteer full time and use it as a way to expand your skills and horizons or even to go global.

The Peace Corps currently has 6,120 volunteers and wants to raise total enrollment to 10,000, if government funding will support that increase. Former Peace Corps volunteers number 140,000, and many have achieved high-level jobs in business and government. A jobs bulletin assists newly returned volunteers in locating jobs or graduate school assistantships. Local groups provide networking opportunities. Geared up for the global marketplace, volunteers come back from their two-year tours with some very salable skills, such as language proficiency and demonstrated ability to adjust to another culture. Businesses and government agencies that are international in focus have welcomed returning volunteers.

Of special interest to mid-career managers is the recent Peace Corps emphasis on small business development in Eastern Europe. Applicants must have three to five years of experience in managing or running their own businesses or must have degrees in business. People contemplating early retirement should know that 10 percent of all current volunteers are over fifty-five.

Susan supercharged her career through volunteerism. At age twenty-four, while she was working full time for a greeting card company, she founded an animal rights organization. She says she picked up valuable business skills, such as how to organize programs, lead meetings, set up budgets, work with suppliers, and make public appearances. The supervisory experience she gained with volunteers cinched her first management position and helped her rise to vice president of a marketing and advertising agency. Handling media relations for her volunteer organization, she turned her career in that direction and now has her own firm. She believes so strongly in volunteering as a career enhancer that she is frequently invited to speak to groups. Her speech is titled, "How a Little Charity Can Do Your Career Good."

Go Play

Turn a hobby into a career? Sounds too good to be true, but if you have a very strong interest outside of work, consider its career possibilities. Many people have found satisfying, lucrative jobs and business ventures by taking their playtime full-time. Of course, like any other career transition, such a move will take some planning, maybe some additional training, and certainly some creativity about how to parlay the skills you play with into the skills you work with—but it can be done.

Lorrie's nine-to-five job was in international hotel marketing, but every spare moment was spent with her dummy, Herman. She is a ventriloquist. Although she and Herman occasionally entertained at parties, she'd never considered a career as a ventriloquist because she didn't want to do a nightclub act. When she and Herman were asked to give a presentation on customer service at a convention, she discovered the world of professional paid speaking. To help her bridge slowly over to her new career, she joined the National Speakers Association where she learned more about how to present and market to business audiences. She took on as many speaking events as she could while still working full time. After one year, she resigned from her job and she and Herman have become a very successful duo on the professional speaking circuit.

Rebecca's joy in life was making African-American dolls. She spent every weekend and evening buying supplies, sewing dolls, and selling the dolls at craft fairs. When a department store offered her a contract for 1,000 dolls, she happily quit her job as an operations manager and employed her mother to sew for her full time. "In the short run, I want my dolls to teach children pride in their African heritage and history," Rebecca says. "Long term, I plan to open a gift shop and sell the crafts of other African-American artists."

Go Moonlight

What a great way to experiment with how to get a fledgling business to fly! Work at it evenings and weekends. See how you like it. See how it likes you. More than 7.5 million Americans work full time but run a part-time business on the side. At the very least, you'll strengthen your identity as a proactive person. If bosses are not threatened by your efforts, they appreciate the go-getters who moonlight and consider them high-energy, flexible employees. At best, you'll learn some new skills and make a little money to bolster your career security. If you really hit the jackpot, you'll find a way to go full time, as you use your skills to serve a hot market niche.

Keep your sideline and mainline jobs separate. Do not use company time or equipment for your own business. Using company resources for your own profit is a good way to get fired.

The three moonlighting activities most acceptable in corporate America while you are still employed are teaching, consulting, and writing. Most employers respect those efforts, and many even support them, even if they discourage employees from moonlighting in more product- or service-oriented areas. Teaching, consulting, and writing also are ideal ways to gain visibility and to establish expertise—both key factors in making career changes or creating a career as an entrepreneur.

David, a director in the engineering department of a large utility company, bought a neighborhood newspaper. As publisher, he set the editorial tone, but left the day-to-day operations to his staff and a cadre of freelancers. Staying abreast of city politics and rubbing elbows with politicians and city planners gave him in-depth knowledge of urban development, a topic he dealt with in his job.

He believes he held his job through successive waves of layoffs because of the expertise he developed as a result of his work with the newspaper.

Go Teach

Teaching is such a traditional profession that people often overlook it. Yet, as a way to expand and explore career options, it can't be beat. If you shudder at the thought of a day alone with twenty-eight fourth graders, think again. Think of all the places teaching takes place: in colleges and graduate schools, in noncredit adult education programs, in employee training programs inside organizations, in technical schools, in communities, in churches. The possible settings are almost endless in our information-focused society.

If you do choose the public school system, explore quick ways to earn your credentials. Most states now offer alternative teacher certification programs to liberal arts graduates, many of them aimed at job-switchers, homemakers returning to work, or retirees. Some allow candidates who are in a hurry to teach even before they receive official state certification.

When Matt's boss said his job as program director at a community college was being abolished due to budget cuts, Matt was surprised. He never expected the college to lay off anyone. He stayed on for another year by taking over the duties of a colleague who resigned when her husband was transferred out of the area. During that year, Matt began to teach in one of the evening programs he'd been managing. He used those credentials to get a few one-day training assignments to teach supervisory skills at local corporations. He took intensive, three-day courses himself to improve his platform skills and knowledge of training design. He joined the American Society for Training and Development and felt confident that becoming a full-time trainer was a real career option for him should he ever need to or want to go in that direction. His efforts paid off unexpectedly when, because of his increased expertise, a large outplacement firm offered him a job training other trainers to teach courses in career development.

As the military began to downsize, Chuck, who had nineteen years of service, set up a smooth transition to his second career, supplemented by his retirement pay. A back-to-basics Marine, who loves and believes in kids, he decided to teach. By taking evening and weekend classes during his last year of active duty, he finished the requirements for his master's degree, a master of arts in teaching. He now teaches math in high school. "I feel like I'm making a real contribution to my community, and I also have the summers free to travel with my wife," he says.

Go Combo

Creating a combo career means combining several possibly very diverse jobs and career option strategies.

Ted, age forth-eight, is chief of court services, full time, for a judicial district in northwestern Kansas.

On the side, he's in the Air Force Reserves. Serving

as a disaster preparedness staff officer during the Gulf War, he taught Saudi Arabians about responses to chemical warfare. Knowing that the military is downsizing, he fireproofed his military career by taking on a second job as admissions liaison officer for the Air Force Academy.

A pilot during the Vietnam War, he still flies. He ferries patients to and from a mental health and chemical dependency treatment facility aboard the hospital's airplane.

With a friend, he also restores antique tractors.

There's more. "Seven or eight guys from Oklahoma come to hunt pheasant every year on my farm," he says. "They're corporate CEOs, and I figure, if bad comes to worse, I could always find a job through one of them."

He's also an expert in handwriting analysis, something he often uses with juvenile clients "to pick up on traits." He also does handwriting analysis for individuals.

And, he could go back to a previous career as a vocational agriculture teacher.

Ted's collection of careers is particularly interesting because it proves you don't have to live in a big city to have lots of career options.

Get going—up, out, back, sideways, over, into a niche, home, south, inland, or global. Consider temping, part-timing, innovating, entreprenuring, franchising, volunteering, turning a hobby into a job, moonlighting, teaching, or combining jobs.

As you explore and expand your options, you will increase the odds that, whatever happens to your job, you'll be able to continue to earn a living—maybe even in a way that's more satisfying to you than the way you do now.

Chapter 10

Link Up with People

''Network? You've got to be kidding! I'm working so hard I don't even have time to get a haircut!'' says Bill, who ''survived'' two downsizings and one merger in the last eighteen months.

Often it's the people who are still employed who have the most difficulty networking and the most to lose by not creating and nurturing a safety net of contacts. Listen to Sherry: ''I wish they'd go ahead and lay me off, if they're going to. Then I'd have time to network. The people who are out of work and looking for a job have it easier. They have time to go to lunch and talk on the phone and be active in professional associations. It must be nice. Meanwhile, I'm stuck, trying to hang on to my job and working sixty hours a week with a bunch of people who are just as scared and depressed as I am.''

Sherry knows she ought to be networking, but she feels trapped by escalating job demands. Unfortunately, most employers no longer reward this kind of commitment with a ''till death do us part'' contract.

Mike found that out the hard way. As the director of human resource development at a major telecommunications firm, he says, ''I should have seen the handwriting on the wall, but I said to myself, 'If you just work long hours and do a good job, you'll be able to ride out the merger and survive the cuts.' So, when I got laid off, I was not only shocked, I had no network! I hadn't been to a professional association meeting in a year, was out of touch with old friends, always said I was too busy when people called to have lunch. I kept telling myself, 'I've just got to keep my nose to the grindstone.' The biggest shock was not that I didn't have a network. I guess I knew that. The biggest shock was that I didn't know how to network. So, I started my job search with two big deficits that took about six months to correct. I had to get a lot better at all those connecting skills, and I had to start from scratch."

Don't let someone else's shoulda, coulda, woulda tale of woe give you a case of the willies, but do recognize that you'll need to strategize your way around three barriers to create your safety net while you're still employed.

Overcome the Barriers

"I don't have time to network," Margaret says.

You're expected to do the jobs of three people (the other two were laid off or quit and weren't replaced) and work overtime to get the job done and show commitment. Sure, it's hard to fit networking into a busy schedule. Think of it like exercising: forecasting the consequences of not doing it can move you into action. Like exercising, once you get into a networking routine, it's more fun, and you'll soon experience the rewards of success. In this chapter, we'll show you how, with an investment of only about three hours a week, you can have a strong network in six months.

"I can't seem to disconnect from my current job enough to feel like networking," says Ted. "I'm mentally and emotionally exhausted. I don't have the energy to reach out to people, and I don't know where to start."

The link-up strategy outlined in this chapter takes the work out of networking. Copy the best networkers. They make creating a circle of contacts a way of life, not something else to put on their "to do" lists. As you use these tried and true skills, you'll find that networking actually powers you up rather than saps your energy.

"I don't know where to network," says SueAnn. "Some professional associations can be bottomless pits, into which you pour endless time and enormous energy. They want you to be on all kinds of committees, and everybody I meet there asks if there are any openings at my company! It feels like I'm not getting enough."

You're right. Choosing which organizations to join and how to get involved are crucial decisions. Many people hear rumors about a layoff and leap into a networking organization without testing the waters first. They write a check for the dues, say "yes" to committee work without really considering how it will add to their visibility or future employability. And then they waste time at networking functions talking about the wrong things.

Use the ideas in this chapter to plan which organizations to join and what to do and say when you get there so you gain the most visibility, contacts, and professional growth. With this know-how, you can create a no-nonsense network that will be the cornerstone of your career security plan.

What's the Net Worth of Your Network?

Taking the Quiz: Any sound strategy begins with an assessment of how you're doing now. Here's a quiz that will help you assess the net worth of your current networking skills. Think about *the last six months* and circle Y for yes and N for no. At the end of this quiz, you'll find instructions for assessing the value of your network.

Y N 1. I see all those informal conversations at business and social events as opportunities to use my small talk skills to build relationships and expand my network.

Y N 2. I know at least fifty people well enough (professionally or in the community) to call and say, "Hi, this is [my name]," and they know who I am and what my capabilities are.

Y N 3. People in my network have referred me to at least ten people who have given me some kind of career or personal information.

Y N 4. I'm comfortable calling friends of friends, and friends of friends of friends to seek information.

Y N 5. I belong to at least four professional or community organizations and am visibly active in them.

Y N 6. I read two trade journals or magazines in my field and two general news publications consistently.

Y N 7. I know people outside of my profession from activities, such as sports, PTA, or volunteer work.

Y N 8. I've taken at least one course or gone to one convention to help me stay current in my field or learn about a new field.

Y N 9. I stay in touch with people I knew and worked with at previous jobs.

Y N 10. I make a point of meeting people outside my organization, profession, or industry, and at all levels of the hierarchy.

Y N 11. At a social or business event, I'm comfortable with introductions and can remember the names of people I meet.

Y N 12. I introduce people to one another at business and social events.

Y N 13. When people ask, "What do you do?" I avoid long, confusing job titles and labels. Instead I tell what I do, simply and vividly, by giving an example of a recent project or success.

Y N 14. I let people know the kinds of problems I can solve, so that they often refer exactly the right kind of work challenges, job leads, or career information to me.

Y N 15. When I talk to people, I usually find up-to-date information on something of professional or personal interest to me.

Y N 16. I talk frequently with others for support, ideas, and resources.

Y N 17. I systematically network with people in my organization who work in other departments, other divisions, and other locations.

Y N 18. I have business cards and enjoy using conversation to look for ways to give or receive information or services so that exchanging cards is valuable and necessary.

Y N 19. I always find a good way to say, "Thank you," when someone gives me information or resources or a referral to someone they know.

Y N 20. I look for ways that my resources and information can help others fulfill their personal and professional goals.

Scoring Yourself: Count how many times you circled Y, then analyze your score.

1–10 Strengthen your career security as you learn the basics of networking. In the past, you may not have felt comfortable networking or may not have been convinced that networking could benefit you. However, you can **learn** how to do it, feel comfortable, and improve your on-the-job performance as well as your long-range career security. Your new skills will pay off quickly.

11–14 You can give and get even more in your professional and personal networks as you develop your networking skills. You've learned some of the basics. Now use the ideas in this chapter to build a stronger foundation and apply your skills in all kinds of situations.

15–17 You have only a few gaps in your network. Look at the questions you answered with Ns. Use the ideas in this chapter to help you strengthen those areas. Your satisfaction with networking varies: sometimes it works and sometimes it doesn't. You can make it work for you, every time.

18–20 Bravo! You're well on the way to experiencing the power of career security through networking. Use the ideas in this chapter to reinforce and polish what you already are doing.

The Link-Up Strategy

Networking is exchanging information, resources, and support in such a way that you build relationships.

What kinds of relationships?

As you think about people, you'll notice that with some you have a more active and reciprocal relationship than with others. If you want to have a closer networking relationship with someone, identify the amount of activity and trust you currently have, then decide what a good next step might be.

Use the targeting diagram on page 202 and the descriptions that follow, starting on page 202, to decide what to do next to build your network. What's the next step you might take with Jon, who currently fits into the acquaintance category, or Molly, whom you'd classify as an associate?

Map out your next moves to build strategic relationships. Get busy, and soon you'll have a safety net that will protect you from becoming a casualty of the economy and will help you ensure your career mobility.

Targeting Diagram

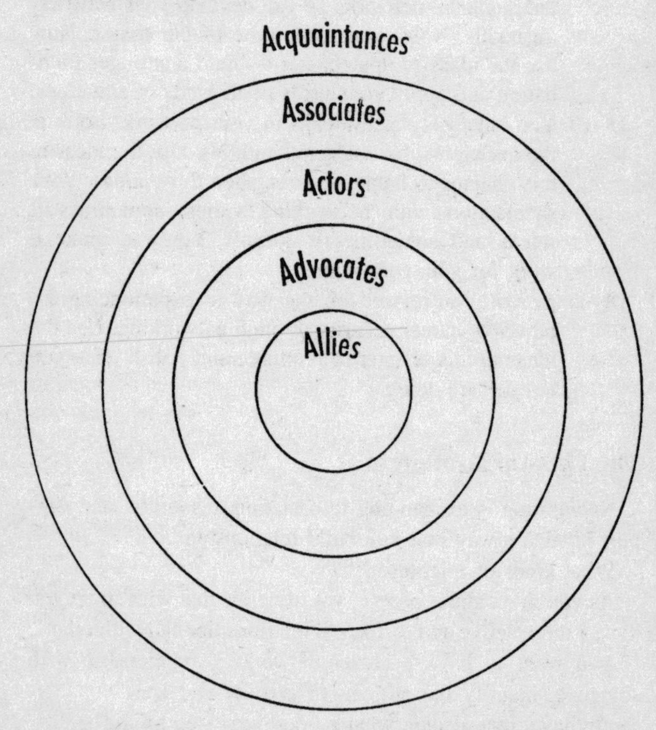

Acquaintances: There's no circle around these folks, because they barely know who you are. You bump into them in the cafeteria or at a Chamber of Commerce event, but you may never see them again. They're a face in a sea of faces; so are you. You're not in their network; they're not in yours. Occasionally, something clicks and you are able to exchange something of value with an acquaintance, but more often than not, your contact is brief and nonproductive. If you know how to encourage repeat encounters and how to follow up with people, some good networking contacts will eventually come from people who begin their interactions with you as acquaintances. However, you usually will have to collaborate to set up repeated contacts with these people before your efforts will pay off. In other words, you will need to become associates, who meet on a regular basis.

Associates: You see these people regularly because you have chosen to join a group that brings you into contact with them at a professional association, an alumni club, or a volunteer activity, for instance. Perhaps both of you actively are pursuing contact with each other outside of any formal group. Now that you have arranged to see each other regularly, you have a chance to teach each other your names and to exhibit your character and competence to each other, as you chair a committee, make meeting announcements, or edit the newsletter. Over time, your associates experience you as someone who is energizing to be with, who can be counted on to come through with what he or she has promised, and who has valuable skills. Simultaneously, you begin to appreciate them. Because of proximity and frequency, you have a ready-made arena in which you can learn more about each others' skills, challenges, and interests. These people no longer say about you, "I think he's an accountant . . . no, maybe he's in computers, or something." Now they say, "He's a systems analyst who's an expert in computer security." You know them equally well. Mutually beneficial exchanges will flourish as you and your contacts become associates.

Actors: Think of actors on a stage. They are in dialogue. Something's happening between them. Actors are the people on your list with whom you are actively exchanging valuable information and resources. You give them leads or tips. They tell you about a resource or introduce you to someone you want to meet. Over time, trust grows, and you become interested in adding to each other's success. Here's where listening generously comes in. Would you like to move from being an associate to being an actor with someone you know? Tune in to what your contact is looking for. Put your antenna up for resources for them. Giving with no strings attached is the best way to invite reciprocity.

Advocates: Advocates are people who go out of their way to find opportunities to refer and recommend you to others for a position on the board, as a possible job candidate, or to emcee the fund-raiser, for instance. They are so confident about your abilities and your integrity that they are willing to put their good names on the line to promote you. Advocates make sure the people you want to meet hear about you before they hear from you. You do the same for them.

Allies: Think of these people as being on your very own board of trustees. They care about your success. They give you advice that you respect because, as your relationship develops, they become experts on you. They keep what you say confidential. They commiserate with you when life gets you down. They give you a nudge when you most need it. They cheer you on in every arena of your life. They celebrate your successes with as much enthusiasm as you do theirs. You play the same roles in their lives. You won't have time to cultive too many relationships to this level, so you must select these people carefully. These relationships are long-term and usually turn into friendships as allies see each other socially, as well as professionally.

CAUTION: You'll be a labeled a "nuisance networker" for sure if, out of enthusiasm or urgency, you violate the natural development of trust in a relationship as shown in the targeting diagram by trying to jump from acquaintance to advocate or ally. Give the people you interact with time to experience your competence and character and take the time to experience theirs before you request assistance that only advocates or allies are willing and able to give. If someone you hardly know calls and asks you for something, like help getting a job interview with one of your valued contacts, you've probably felt uneasy. That discomfort is easy to explain: You are not willing to put your good name on the line with your contact to promote someone you don't know. Yet, this kind of nuisance networking happens all the time. If someone does try to use you, say, "I'm sorry, but I can't possibly recommend someone I don't know for that job." If you want to help the person who has called, say, "Why don't we get together and talk at the next meeting of my professional association? You are welcome to make a reservation. When you arrive, ask anyone you meet to point me out to you. I'll be happy to meet you and we can begin to get acquainted."

As you implement the ideas in this chapter, you will create mutually beneficial relationships that move naturally and comfortably from acquaintance relationships to associate relationships. As you use networking occasions as opportunities for you and your contact to teach each other about yourselves and your capabilities and character and to trade valuable information with each other, you will begin to progress into more active relationships. You will find that, with some effort, you and your contacts can become actors, or even advocates, and finally allies.

Networking know-how can make you fireproof if you know and use the 6 × 6 × 6 formula:

6 skills	You'll use six skills to make great connections.
6 months	It takes about six months to create a network from scratch.
6 organizations	You must know people and be known in six organizations to experience your net working.

Six Skills

Any project can seem overwhelming if you don't know the steps or have some guidelines. Remember the first time you tried to wallpaper a room or use the graphics package on your computer without reading the manual first? Like any other activity, once you invest some time in perfecting the skills, the rewards multiply. Even people who were born with the gift of gab have used these skills to enhance their abilities to make great connections.

1. Show Up

You can show up without showing off. Unfortunately, when it comes to social and business events, it sometimes feels as if we're caught back at the eighth grade dance. Remember the eighth grade dance? It was the first social situation in which you were on your own and supposed to be adept. The number one rule was "Be cool! Don't look like you like anybody or want anything." When you bring that mind-set to new or stressful situations like a professional association meeting, the voice inside your head says things like, Nobody will want to talk to me. I know I won't be able to think of anything interesting to say. I never can remember names.

Well, we're not at the eighth grade dance anymore. Great connectors replace those sabotaging thoughts with encouraging self-prophecies like, I wonder who I'll meet here tonight? I bet I can remember five people's names. Lots of good things have come my way when I've just leaped in and talked to people.

Let your natural excitement and curiosity about life shine through. Smile. Move energetically and with purpose. Ask questions. Volunteer information. Look for ways to contribute your ideas and expertise to others. That's the way to show up.

2. Meet and Greet

You have only two or three minutes to make a memorable first connection with people you meet. Although we often rush through introductions hoping to get on to the good stuff, the truth is, exchanging names and getting clear on what you each do *is* the good stuff. Here's how to handle introductions so that the conversation gets off to a good start.

The Name Game—Linger Longer: It's your responsibility to help people to remember your name. Think ahead of time how you can teach people your name and make it stick in their minds.

"Hi, I'm Fred Johnson—Fred, like in Fred Astaire."

"Hello, I'm Rona. It's like Mona, but spelled with an R."

"Hi, I'm Lydia, but you can call me Dee. It got shortened a long time ago, and I decided I like it."

If someone says to you, "Oh, I never can remember names," that's your cue to make your name memorable. Be ready. Say, "Mine's easy to remember. It's Burt, spelled with a U," or "It's Helena. That means light."

When you are introduced to someone, slow down. Linger longer in the conversation about your contact's name. Ask how it's spelled or what it means. Make a connection out loud.

"Is that M-a-r-y or M-e-r-r-y?"

"Hi, William. Do you go by William or Bill?"

"Nice to meet you, Phil. That's my brother's name. That'll be easy for me to remember."

Introductions—Use the Best/Test: Tell what you do, not what you are. Think of one sentence that tells what you do best or what you want people to remember about you. That's your *best.* Then give a short example that provides a testimonial of your success. That's your *test.* Avoid long, jargon-filled job titles. Tell what you do in such a way that it's a conversation starter and add an example of a recent success or project.

Bill is a biochemist, whose job is consumer education. When someone asks him, "What do you do?" he introduces himself, especially when he's not with other scientists, by saying, "I help people read between the lines on the soup can labels. I just testified at a congressional subcommittee on how companies tell—or don't tell—us about the salt in our food."

Maria is a health care grants administrator and policy specialist with the federal government. She uses the best/test, saying, "I look at how we spend money to prevent and cure arthritis and see if we can get more for our tax dollars. Last year, I was able to reduce the money going for overhead and double the amount of money spent to find a cure."

Your introduction will vary depending on the event and the

audience. How you say what you do at a backyard barbecue probably will be different from what you say at a professional conference. But in both settings, the idea is to get into conversation about what you do and what the other person does. So, talk in pictures, describe activities, tell what kinds of problems you solve. When the person you're meeting gives you a job title full of acronyms and labels, you can move the conversation ahead by asking, "What's a typical day like in your work?" or "How did you first get interested in that?" or even "If I followed you around for a day, what would we be doing?"

3. Create an Agenda

Vocalist Roberta Flack was once asked, "What makes a great singer?" She replied, "You've got to know where your song comes from." The same is true with the small talk that's at the heart of networking. It's got to come from someplace. Without a purpose, small talk becomes just pleasant schmoozing, chatting about the ball game, or commiserating about the weather. That may pass the time, but it's not networking.

Before you head out to any gathering where you might be able to link up with people, create an agenda for yourself. An agenda is simply a list of what you're looking for and what you're willing to give to others. Draw from a wide range of personal and professional interests to find topics you want to talk about.

Look at these examples of very specific conversation-starting agenda items, then make your own list. Until agenda-setting becomes automatic for you, put your list on paper and stick the note in your pocket. Even if you don't refer to it during the event, having it there will give you confidence and remind you that you're setting out to get and give valuable information.

What I Have to Give *(information, expertise, enthusiasms, resources)*	**What I Want to Get** *(find, learn, connect with, have more of, solve)*
New software package for keeping track of contacts	How to get articles accepted by professional journals

What I Have to Give	**What I Want to Get**
Wedding planning resources and ''dos and don'ts''	How to choose a puppy or dog for my ten-year-old
Fun things to do while vacationing in Maine	A good course on how to give a speech or a presentation.
Job bank run by my professional association	New ways to influence people to see the importance of management training in our company
How to do an employee satisfaction survey	A good piano teacher

Turning into what's on your ever-changing agenda gives small talk a purpose. Without a purpose, there's no exchange of resources and information. If there's no exchange, the networking relationship never develops. The next time you meet, you have to start all over again. When you know what you have to give and what you'd like to learn or connect with, then the chance to talk with people turns into an exciting search.

Notice that if you always know what's on your agenda, you'll never be at a loss for words. You'll avoid the tired, old routine that gives small talk a bad name:

''How are you?''

''Not bad.''

''What's new?''

''Not much.''

Instead, be prepared to be spontaneous. Respond to ''What's new?'' by telling what's on your agenda. ''I've just set up a job bank for the professional association I belong to,'' says Bob. ''I've met some wonderful people and learned some amazing things about the job market in this city,'' or ''Well, I've recently decided that it's never too late to learn to play the piano. I'm looking for a teacher. Do you know anyone who'll take on somebody who only got to the middle of Book

Three twenty-five years ago, but who now desperately wants another chance?'' asks Barbara.

Your conversations will become explorations of how you can help each other. Exchanges create relationships of trust, even if the conversation is about piano lessons or the best place to trout fish. Your safety net will expand each time you're able to give something away. Give generously—more than you get. Then, when you need something, you'll feel more comfortable asking for it, and people will be much more receptive to your requests for help. If you think there is even the tiniest possibility that your job could disappear, **now** is the time to build relationships by giving and giving and giving some more. If you can't discover what people are looking for, ask. Everybody's looking for something!

''How can I help you?''

''Is there some kind of information or resource I could help you find?''

''What's your big challenge at work in the next few months?''

The reciprocity principle will kick in. Research on this phenomenon of human nature verifies that when you give people something, they just naturally try to find ways to help you in return. Studies show that most people work hard to give back more than they received.

4. Tap into the Six-Million-People Network

Your potential network is bigger, more powerful, and more far-reaching than you may realize. Do you know fifty people? Most people have many more friends and acquaintances than that. But, let's be conservative. If each of those people knows fifty people, you now know 2,500 people who are friends of friends. If each of those people knows fifty people, you now know 125,000 people who are friends of friends of friends. If each of those people knows fifty people, you now have access to more than six million people. Do you think that pool is large enough to connect you with whatever resource, idea, or person you're looking for?

As you pursue this link-up strategy to create your safety net, you'll become skilled at tapping into the power of other people's networks. When Sally, a New Yorker, realized her company was going to move its corporate headquarters to Kansas City in two years, she told her neighbor Rick she wanted to find a job that would allow her to stay in New York. He arranged a meeting between Sally and June, the sales manager at a company he used to work for. A few months later, when that company expanded its sales division, Sally was called for an interview and was able to change jobs before her company's move got under way.

What would your reaction be if we asked you to write down all the people in your network? Some people say, "Well, that's easy. There are four people!" Others say, "You've got to be kidding. That would take hours!" Whether you can think of only a few or hundreds, we do recommend you take the time now to list the people in your network. After you do it, we'll tell you why. To jog your memory, here are several categories:

- People at work, throughout the organization
- Colleagues from previous workplaces
- Customers, suppliers
- Peers and leaders in professional associations
- People in civic, community, or religious organizations
- Relatives
- Neighbors, past and present
- Professors, instructors, fellow students, past teachers, fellow alumni, sorority or fraternity contacts
- Friends and acquaintances from leisure-time activities
- Professionals who serve you, like your dentist
- People you know through your parents or your kids

Do you remember the old saying, "It's not what you know, it's who you know?" Well, what you know is important. The more you know, the more you have to give away. The more you're seen as an expert, the more people turn to you if they have a question, whether it's about how to grow orchids or how to motivate the twenty-something workforce. And who you know is important because those are the people you'll call on when you're up against a challenge, whether it's how to find a consultant to lead a team-building session for your staff or what's the best place to stay when you take the kids to Disney World. But far more important than what you know or who you know is who knows you. When an opportunity or need comes up, how many people on the list you just made know your skills, abilities, and challenges so well that your name pops up in their mental Rolodex, and they almost automatically say, "Call Todd" or "I'll send this to Karen. It might be a job lead for her." Who knows you that well?

Look at your list of people and ask yourself these questions to tap into the power of the six-million-people safety net.

How many people do I want to know me? Given my profession or industry and my current career security, how many people would I like to have who know what I'm looking for in the way of opportunities and resources? In our fireproofing and networking workshops, we've seen people aim for as few as 10 and as many as 250. When layoffs loom, you will definitely need a higher goal than 10 people. Decide for yourself, and circle those names on your list. If the names aren't on your list, write down the kinds of people you'd like to meet and think about where to find them. As Author Tom Peters reminds us, "The new security resides in the network you're a part of . . . not your logo."

How am I going to become known to the people whose names I've circled? Become more active in trade or professional associations? Write an article for a magazine or newsletter? Schedule lunches with old friends and coworkers? Offer to give a speech on my speciality at a professional conference? Attend more events at my workplace (retirement dinners, awards luncheons, United Way rallies, etc.)? Stop reading my mail before meetings and start getting to know people?

5. Practice the Protocol

Good networkers stand out in a crowd for all the right reasons: their expertise, their generosity, and their friendliness. When it comes to etiquette, however, they blend in. They follow the customs of the groups they circulate in; they observe the rules of the tribe.

Put on your sociologist's hat and observe the behavior of various groups. How long do people chat before moving on? What are accepted ways of saying thank you when someone shares a resource? How do people ask for a follow-up meeting with someone they meet? What are the rules about touching and hugging? Following the old edict "When in Rome, do as the Romans do" will add to your comfort level and help you gain respect. We suggest these guidelines for three practices people in our workshops have many questions about.

Handing Out Your Business Cards: We've heard it described as "a game of business bumper cars." People whiz frantically around the room banging into people and handing out business cards under the illusion that they're networking.

You know what happens when someone gives you his business card too soon. You get home, glance at it, and think, "I wonder who he was?" and you toss the card into the wastebasket.

To avoid having your card end up in the circular file, pour your energy into the conversation first. Look for connections. Ted has used a voice mail system your organization is considering? Ask for his card and for permission to call him later to ask how he likes the system. You have contacts in San Francisco where Louisa is going to relocate next month? Give her your card and ask for hers. Suggest that she call you after you've had a chance to put your hands on the names and addresses of those contacts.

Those are reasons to exchange business cards. When you talk about what's on your agenda and listen for what's on other people's agendas, a cardboard connection turns into a great connection. You can even write a reminder on the card about the best time to call or what you've promised to send that person. By the way, in Japan, a business card is considered an extension of oneself. To write on it is a grave insult. That's another example of how important it is to know the protocols of the people you meet.

Joining Groups of People Who Are Already Talking: Entering a room full of people can give even the most gregarious person pause. "What if no one talks to me?" "What if I can't think of anything to say?"

Plan ahead just how you'll introduce yourself and what's on your agenda. Then, as you enter the room, take a moment to look around. Is someone standing alone? Striking up a conversation with one person may be easier than walking up to a group.

On the other hand, you can join groups easily and comfortably. Here's how. Don't choose a group whose energy is too high or exuberant. They don't need you! Don't choose one that's too quiet or intimate. You could be interrupting something private. Decide where to enter the group, and use eye contact and body language to signal your intention. To create an opening, lightly touch the elbow of the person standing where you want to enter. Smile and give your full attention to the person who is talking. Three cheers for the savvy person in the group who smiles back or turns briefly to you and says, "Joe is just telling us about his new job." When that topic winds down, you can ask "How do you all know each other?" They'll either tell you, or they'll say, "We don't." And introductions can begin.

If the conversation stops the minute you join the group, its possible you interrupted something private. If you think that's the case, say, "Looks like I better catch you later," or "Sorry, I seem to have interrupted something." However, it's much more likely that the group's interest in what they were talking about had waned, and they were desperately hoping you'd bring some new energy and new topics, so be ready with something on your agenda.

If the organization is new to you, don't try to pretend you're an old hand; make the most of being a newcomer. Say, "This is my first time here. Tell me more about the meetings," or "What do you like best about being a member?" or "What happens next? I've never been here before," or "I'm hoping to meet other people who are in media relations. Can you think of anyone?" People love to be helpful if asked directly.

Remember, everyone's a bit nervous when they are with

strangers. Focus on putting others at ease by introducing people to each other and helping to make the event a success. Act like a host or hostess, not a guest. If the speaker is passing out materials before the meeting, jump up and help. If the name tags arrived late, offer to take them around to people. Activity creates conversation, so get active.

Saying Thank You: Mom was right. Thank-yous are important. When an association management executive finally got the perfect job offer, the first thing she did to celebrate was to call her florist and have flowers sent to the four people who had helped her the most during her six-month search. She wanted them to share in her excitement, and she found an unusual way to say thanks and announce her success. There are many kinds of thanks to choose from: a handwritten note, a formal letter on office stationary, a phone call, an invitation to lunch, access to a resource from your network. Knowing you can't ever make networking exchanges exactly equal, what's even better is to show appreciation in unique and memorable ways.

6. Tune into the Quiet Side

Good networkers don't do all the talking. There's a quiet side to networking, called—you guessed it—listening. Listen generously. Listen for other people's agendas. Listen with an ear for how you can contribute to their success. Jay Levinson, the guerilla marketing guru, advises, "Networking is not a time to toot your own trombone, but to ask questions, listen attentively to the answers, and keep your marketing radar attuned to the presence of problems." Be seriously curious. You'll get information on business trends and solutions to challenges you face. Think back over your life. Hasn't most of the best information come from people, not print? The name of a good day care center for your two-year-old, how to get around all the red tape in procurement, and the name of a good temporary help firm when you needed to increase your staff to meet a peak demand might all be found by word of mouth.

Here are just a few open-ended questions to ask that are guaranteed to get other people talking.

- "How did you first get interested in that?"
- "Where do you think the technology (company, industry, program, city) will be ten years from now?"
- "What was your role in the project?"
- "What's your advice to someone like me who wants to get more involved in that?"
- "What was the high point for you?"
- "What is your biggest challenge in the next six months?"
- "What's a typical day like for you?"

As you listen for other people's enthusiasms and challenges, you may find ways you can help them with your resources and your network. Also be alert for resources that will help you with your agenda. If it's appropriate, offer or ask for help. Then, be sure to follow up. Do what you say you're going to do. Don't abuse networking situations by doing a hard sell or cornering people. When you see a connection, exchange cards. Say, "I'd like to call you this week to get that phone number. Is Tuesday a good day to reach you?" or "It sounds as if we have more to talk about. How about meeting for breakfast next Wednesday?"

Six Months

How long does it take to build a network? Your network will never be finished. You'll always be building new relationships and renewing old ones. That's why it's important to integrate connecting into your lifestyle and to streamline—and probably computerize—the process of reconnecting.

Make Networking a Way of Life

"I tried networking last Thursday and nothing happened," says Janice in frustration. Of course not: It's a process, not an event. Sure, you have to begin by putting specific events on your calendar, but the goal is to make connecting a way of life. It takes at least six months to cultivate a bountiful network. Not every attempt to reach out succeeds. Yet, over time, with enough contacts and lots of attention and patience, your network will begin to have a dramatic impact on your life.

If you invest about three hours a week for six months in networking activities, you can create a viable safety net. If you neglect any relationship, however, it will wither. It doesn't work to network frantically for a period of time and then stop. You will need to build and nurture relationships continuously. Find ways to reconnect, follow up, and stay in touch. If you do, then you'll feel less vulnerable in your job or in the job market because you'll always be in touch with a wealth of new ideas, referrals, hot information, support, and resources.

What exactly would you do if you invested three hours a week? George networks effectively. We asked him to explain some items on his July calendar.

July 1 Lunch with Sam, former employee who started his own company. Talked market trends and new product ideas. (1½ hours)

July 9 Sent newspaper article on a new conference center to Susan in purchasing. She had mentioned wanting to have an off-site retreat with her staff. (2 minutes)

July 13 Attended lunch meeting of professional association. Talked to three people I know and met four new people. Will follow up with Tom Ellis, whose organization is expanding. Will ask Bob Morton in Orlando to call Dana, whose colleague is looking for a consultant there. (2½ hours)

July 14 Called Louise, a long-time acquaintance in a related industry, to say "Congratulations" on her promotion and to ask about renting her beach house for the weekend. (15 minutes)
Called neighbor to let him know that my friend Louise, who just got promoted, is interviewing people to fill her former job. (5 minutes)

July 17 Represented my company at a two-day conference in New York. Had breakfast with executive search firm representative my sister-in-law knows, introduced noted speaker to audience of 150 then took her to lunch, went to a networking party hosted by a state in which I might want to retire eight years from now. Ran into old friend from college who lives in New York, did an information interview with his boss to find out about their organization. (5 hours)

July 24 Sent Susan (on program committee of professional association) an article by a convention speaker and recommended inviting him to present a workshop for our local chapter (10 minutes)

During July, George spent about ten hours building networking relationships with a wide circle of people, both inside and outside his company, within his speciality and beyond his profession. Of course, as any savvy networker knows, every chance meeting can become an appointment if you've thought ahead of time about what resources and ideas you're looking for and if you're in touch with what you have that can be of help to others. Life is a networking event; you don't need to wait for a convention or formal meeting with someone.

As networking becomes a way of life rather than something you do at a professional meeting, it becomes ridiculous to say, "I'll spend six hours this month in networking activities." You can develop contacts everywhere and anywhere. A study for Boeing Company reports that when airline passengers got out from behind their briefcases and talked to their seat mates, they often made valuable contacts. Twenty-four percent of those queried said they had developed a customer contact or business relationship after chatting with the person next to them on a trip.

Get Current with Electronic Networks

Are the business cards you collected last week buried under stacks of papers? Do you wonder how you'll ever remember all the fascinating facts you learned about the people you met yesterday? Did you last update your Rolodex in 1987? Don't despair! An electronic tool of the Information Age makes it easy to keep current with contacts. It's called contact management software, and there are as many varieties on the market as there are breakfast cereals.

Used for years by people in sales to keep track of customers and prospects, this software is much more than a computerized Rolodex. It's a package that organizes the information you want to remember about the people in your organization, as well as suppliers, customers, people at previous workplaces, friends, colleagues in your professional association, and anyone else you meet.

Each name you enter in the database can be coded in a variety of ways so that you can pull the information out in all sorts of formats. Wonder who you know in Atlanta? The program can give you a list. Want to know who you know who works in an association? No problem. Wish you had a list of everybody you met at the conference two years ago? Easy. Sure, it takes a moment to enter whatever you decide is basic information like name, title, company, address, phone and fax, and where you met, but once that's in, it's easy to update the file after each contact.

Most packages have lots of other features, too, such as phone dialer, zip code verification, scheduler, day planner, phone message system, and mail merge. Often you can customize the layout of the data on the screen. Shop around for the software that meets your needs.

We recommend that you keep a copy of your professional and personal database on your home computer. It's tangible evidence that your career belongs to you and that one of its most precious assets is your network. Keeping your contact management software at home also reminds you that your career is alive and well outside of the hallowed halls of the organization. On a harsher note, it's sad but true that sometimes being laid off means being locked out. You might immediately lose access to your office. If you have your contact list, electronic or on paper, only at the office, then you have to begin all over again to collect names, addresses, and information for your networking database. Fireproof your electronic Rolodex. Build it at home and regularly make a backup copy so there's no way you can lose it.

Put networking on your calendar, every day. Take every opportunity to meet people, be helpful to them, and let them know you. Use your lunch hour to cultivate new relationships and reconnect with existing contacts. Do not allow your present job to fill every waking moment. Organize your database so you can keep up with your contacts.

Six Organizations

In the next six months, you'll use your six skills in six target organizations or arenas. Now, don't panic! If six sounds like a lot when you have no time, count up your six this way.

1. Network Where You Work

In organizations exploding with change and caught in the constant pressure to attend to the bottom line, strangely enough, people often undervalue building relationships and making contacts internally. "We don't have time to waste time talking!" said John. It doesn't have to be a waste of time. Use your internal network to break down barriers between departments and functional areas. Use it to find solutions to problems, new ways to approach challenges. Use it to improve productivity. Use it to build coalitions and teams.

You'll have more influence in your current job if you realize that "the organization chart is not the business," as Geary Rummler and Alan Brache point out in their book *Improving Performance: How to Manage the White Space on the Organization Chart.* They go on to say, "The greatest opportunities for improvement often lie in the white spaces between the boxes on the chart—in the functional and interpersonal interface—those points where the baton is being passed from one department to another or from one individual to another.''

Establish your reputation as a person who listens to discover how to help others and who knows what's on his ever-changing agenda. Networking helps you get things done in the bureaucracy. Do you call the mail room when you have a missing package or do you call *Jim* in the mailroom? Jim, who is going to college at night and likes to scuba dive and is an expert photographer? It takes only a minute to converse with people and establish relationships that cut red tape and unclog bureaucratic bottlenecks.

Get to know people in other departments. Marcia, in corporate communications, gained valuable information and contacts for her career change to training and consulting because she took the time to get to know people in human resource development. Look for adjacent skills you can learn in case your department is phased out or relocated. When Jorge found out that the accounting department was being moved to regional offices in Houston, he was able, by emphasizing his recognized skills as a manager, to move into a mid-level job in purchasing. In these kinds of shuffles, it's who knows you that counts.

2 and 3. Network in Your Two Professional Groups

You can't join a network. You can't buy a network. You can't sign a membership form, pay your dues and say, ''Okay, I have a network.'' Joining is only the first step—the ticket to get on the train. It's your choice whether to sleep through the whole ride or hop into the engineer's seat and make things happen. Make sure you're on the right train, one that's heading for your destination. Network actively in two professional associations. Choose carefully which organizations to join. Look for one group where many members have the same skills you have. Martin, who handled marketing and advertising for a large hospital, joined the Advertising Club. Look for another organization that focuses on a single industry. Martin also joined a group of hospital public relations people.

Your time and money are valuable. Sample a few programs and events. Peruse the newsletter. Then assess an organization's value to you by asking these questions.

- Are respected professionals from my field among the members?
- How many members are there? Would I be better off joining a large, well-established group or a small group in which I can be more visible and move more quickly into a leadership position?
- Am I enthusiastic about the group's mission?
- What do other people say about this group?
- Is there a good networking culture at meetings? Does the group welcome newcomers? Are people talking about their agendas or the weather?
- Are programs valuable? Do the topics provide professional development at my level?
- Are members people I'd call peers? Are they people with whom I could build support networks and special interest groups?
- Will my organization pay my dues and support my participation? If not, will the organization be worth the money it will cost me? Can I find ways to participate, even if my organization or my boss is unenthusiastic?
- How readily could I move into leadership roles that would give me visibility and career experience?

Once you've decided on the groups to join, here are questions to help you decide how to participate.

- What are my goals here? To learn the basics in a new career field? To meet people in the industry? To build my confidence as a public speaker?
- What do I have to offer the group and the individuals? My writing expertise? My contacts with top-notch speakers? My fund-raising abilities?

- To whom do I want to become known in the group, and for what skills and qualities?
- Am I looking for learning or leadership or a little of both?

The group will benefit and you will, too, if you get clear on the answers to these questions before you agree to chair the membership committee or edit the newsletter. Talk to people who've been members for a while. Read several past newsletters. Scan the membership directory. Remind yourself that you are about to place a very talented person—yourself—in a key position. Take your membership seriously.

4. Network Outside Your Organization

Build relationships with suppliers, customers, or people in related industries or fields you may want to move into or continue to serve.

Jake sells computer software to large accounting firms. He belongs to a sales and marketing professional association, of course, but he also belongs to an association for accountants and CPAs. As a trainer for a large consulting firm, Marla belongs to a health care educators' association because 40 percent of her business comes from that industry. By building relationships in these informal settings, Jake and Marla are expanding their "who knows me" circle where it counts.

Nancy and Eugenie, both bank tellers, hope to open a day care center together. To learn how to proceed with their business idea, they joined a local chapter of the Association of Home-Based Businesses.

5. Network in Your Life

Mingle with people you like and people who share common interests. Follow your interests and participate in activities that are a natural part of your life. These groups could be your aerobic dancing class or your church choir or the pottery class you take on Tuesday evenings.

Fraternity or sorority alumni groups and college alumni

groups could be on your list. They take little time—many meet only quarterly or even annually—but the old school tie is a strong one.

6. Network in the Community

Join one community or civic organization. Developing a circle of contacts in your community adds to your safety net in many ways. You learn about community trends and resources. You expand your knowledge of other industries and businesses and how changes in them may impact your work life. You build supportive relationships that transcend your job title.

Finally, don't forget to network in your life. Everybody you know and meet can be an important part of your network—even Uncle Fred who retired three years ago, even the guy down the street with whom you trade tools every once in a while, even your daughter's swim coach.

Make connecting with people a way of life, rather than a chore.

- At your son's soccer team practices
- With other volunteers at a homeless shelter
- With neighbors at the block party
- With other parents on a hike with your son's Boy Scout troop
- On a weekend trip with your sailing club

When you share your enthusiasm and goals and are genuinely interested in others, you're networking. Never go anywhere without an agenda. When you're aboveboard with your agenda, and there's no mystery, then there's no manipulation. When you say to Bill, a fellow sailing club member, "I'm curious about how you like your work in training and development, because my job in customer service is being phased out, and I'm thinking of a change," then he'll be able to decide if and how to help you in a way that's comfortable for him. Networking is not using people, it's building valuable relationships with people. You must create these relationships exchange by exchange, over a period of time. If you constantly give more than you get, you are networking the right way, you are maintaining your safety net, and best of all you are linked up.

Part III

Action: Fireproof Yourself

Chapter 11

Craft Your Plan and Put It to Work

In chapters 1 through 5, you confronted the terrible truths about job security and learned how layoffs are a part of life. You learned:

- How career management can ensure your future security
- How various forces are causing layoffs and how job risk can be assessed
- How work is wrongly equated with worth and how to create new values to put work in its place
- How the language of layoffs influences those who are let go and those who remain
- How layoff notifications are handled and how to move through the cycle of emotions that job loss stirs up

In chapters 6 through 10, you read about the five strategies for fireproofing your career. You learned:

- How psychological self-employment anchors career security
- How financial self-management establishes career flexibility and freedom from anxiety

- How lifelong education ensures future employability
- How multiple options lead to adjacent or new careers
- How professional and personal relationships create a strong safety net

If you merely read, but do not act on, the prescriptions in this book, your anxiety will only intensify, so take time now to craft your plan and put it into action.

Making Space

Get organized and acquire the tools and equipment you will need to manage your career, outside your current workplace. Set up a home office and make it your career management command post. Your space may be a whole room, a corner of your bedroom, or even a desk in the kitchen. Creating and outfitting your space will improve your ability to take charge and get on with the tasks at hand.

''I knew I might be laid off,'' said Shirley. ''I wish I had thought to outfit an office at home before it happened so I had someplace to go, someplace to be, after it happened. If I had set up a space of my own, I know I would have gone through all those beginning stages of panic and loss—and on to productive job search activities—much more quickly. As it was, I had to figure out what kind of answering machine to buy, paint my bookcase, and learn how to use my contact management software before I could even begin to look for a job.''

Consider what office equipment (computer, fax, phone, photocopy machine, etc.) you would want in your home office if you were unemployed for some period of time. If you can't imagine existing without these tools, part of your fireproofing challenge will be to figure out exactly what you need and how to buy it in the near future.

In the beginning, you'll need at least this basic equipment: a desk, a file cabinet, and a business card or address file, and probably a computer.

''One of the worst things for me about being laid off was

losing my high-powered computer,'' said Ken. ''I had decided not to buy one for my home office because I always said to myself, 'It'll never be as good as the one I have at work.' So, when I was laid off, I spent time shopping around, deciding what to buy, then more time waiting for the equipment to arrive, and still more time setting it all up. If I'd had my home system up and running, I could have started my job search activities a lot sooner.''

Look through everything in your office at work. Bring home any relevant career materials or resources, or copies of these documents. Being in custody of this evidence of your accomplishments builds your sense of being psychologically self-employed. Remember, you might not be allowed to or have time to remove what you want to take with you from your office once you've been notified that you are no longer employed. When some companies have laid people off, they have not even been allowed to remove their briefcases, and only the most obvious personal belongings, like family photos and framed certificates, were packed up and shipped to them.

Here's a checklist of what to take home. You may be able to think of other things that are pertinent to your situation or profession.

- Resumé (updated)
- Performance evaluations
- Information on your job history and a copy of past and present job descriptions
- Letters of praise
- Samples of your best work
- A comprehensive list of training courses you've taken and participant rosters and course manuals
- A copy of important addresses and phone numbers, on disk or on paper
- Membership directories, such as those from your professional association
- Benefits information

Check this list periodically and take items to your home office frequently so that your home resources are always up to date.

Just a reminder: Don't remove anything that doesn't belong to you. Companies are cracking down on theft of intellectual property, such as market data, strategic marketing plans, customer lists—anything that is sensitive, confidential, or proprietary.

Getting Down to Business

Now that you've read this book and have a deeper understanding of what career security is all about, a good way to customize your plan to your needs is to turn back to the career security profile on page 16 and retake this self-assessment quiz.

Forgive yourself if you fudged some of the answers the first time around, hoping that your industry or company would bounce back or figuring that you'd pay off your credit card debt in a couple of months. Free-floating anxiety and wishful thinking can give a rose-colored tint to even the most desperate situation. Many people in our workshops have confessed how hard it is to face the signs of diminishing career security. After they knew more about the entire subject of job security, they were more able to answer the quiz realistically. So, take it again.

For each of the five security strategies—Liberate Your Mind, Line Up Your Finances, Learn for Mastery, Lean Out of Specialization, and Link Up with People—do the following: Examine your current status. Use your responses on the career security profile to analyze where you are and what deficiencies or concerns you have. Begin to work on the area or areas where you are most vulnerable.

To craft your plan, use the following action steps for each chapter as a guide. Pick steps you want to work on, then prioritize them. You many not need to work through all of the action steps; there may be some that you have already handled effectively. On the other hand, you may need to develop additional action steps to fit your particular situation.

Enlist Your Partner

If you haven't already talked with your spouse about the ideas in this book, now's the time to get that person on board. Ask your spouse to read this book. Then you will be able to work together on your plans for increasing your career security.

Wisdom consists of the anticipating of consequences.

NORMAN COUSINS

Only some of us can learn from other people's mistakes. . . . The rest of us have to be the other people.

ANONYMOUS

It wasn't raining when Noah built the ark.

HOWARD RUFF

Chapter One: Running Scared

ACTION STEPS

1. Talk with people you know who have been laid off. Ask for their advice. Give them your support in whatever way you can.
2. Write briefly what motivated you to read this book.
3. Using a scale of one (not very) to ten (extremely), rate your level of apprehension about losing your job. Can you explain exactly why you feel the way you do?
4. Create a support group, two to five other people who also are working on fireproofing their careers. Select these people carefully. Make a conscious decision about whether to include people from your own workplace. You may want to include some people who work in a career field you might like to explore. Get together regularly to encourage each other as you create and implement your plans.

The tools of the mind become burdens when the environment which made them necessary no longer exists.

HENRI BERGSON

People are always blaming their circumstances for what they are. I don't believe in circumstances. The people who get on in this world are the people who get up and look for the circumstances they want, and, if they can't find them, make them.

GEORGE BERNARD SHAW

Chapter Two: Job Insecurity

ACTION STEPS

1. What are your assumptions about work? Consider the list on page 25. Are these statements part of your belief system? Do other beliefs occur to you?
2. Assess the risk of your current job by using the questions on pages 37 through 43 to look at

    - Your industry
    - Your company
    - Your job type
    - Your own job
    - Your geographic location
    - Your personal attributes and assets

3. As you consider your own situation, have you seen any of the warning signs listed on page 41?
4. Challenge yourself to pay more attention to magazine and newspaper articles on topics that are mentioned in this chapter. Also, read more about your particular industry, your company, and your job type.
5. Get to know some executive recruiters. If you don't know how to do this, ask others in your industry and people you know from professional associations whom to contact and how to do it. Many headhunters prefer that you be recommended to them by someone already on their rosters.
6. Get information about any employment agencies that handle temporary or part-time professionals in your field.

One must raise the self by the self
And not let the self sink down
For the self's only friend is the self
And the self is the self's one enemy.

Bhagavad-Gita

Don't be afraid to take a big step if one is indicated; you can't cross a chasm in two small jumps.

WILLIAM LLOYD GEORGE

There is only one success—to spend your life in your own way.

CHRISTOPHER MORLEY

Most powerful is he who has himself in his own power.

SENECA

People often say that this or that person has not yet found himself. But the self is not something that one finds. It is something that one creates.

THOMAS SZASZ

Chapter Three: More Than a Paycheck

ACTION STEPS

1. Talk with your parents and grandparent about the role of work in their lives. What ideas about work do you want to hang on to? What ideas about work would you like to change?
2. Notice how people answer the question, "What do you do?"
3. Notice the feelings you have as you say what you do.
4. Think about the criteria you use to judge the worth of yourself and others.
5. Following the directions on page 51 to 54, transform negative statements from your critic into positive ones for your coach to say. Monitor your use of the "I can'ts," the "I shoulds," the "I'm going to try tos," and the "I want tos."
6. For one month, keep track of exactly how many hours you work every day. Decide how you are going to determine if your employer is making excessive demands on your time. Do you think that you and other employees are volunteering to work longer hours because of layoff anxiety? What can you do to limit the time you spend at work?
7. Take a look at the consequences of putting in excessive overtime on page 55. Do any of the items on the list apply to you? What can you do to change things?
8. How much of your identity comes from your job? What other identity could you develop? List any other identities you already have and would like to strengthen.
9. Examine your values. What do you believe about the place of work in your life?

Survivor—The cruelest of all afflictions.

CHATEAUBRIAND

Words are really a mask. They rarely express the true meaning; in fact, they tend to hide it.

HERMANN HESSE

Words not only affect us temporarily; they change us, they socialize or unsocialize us.

DAVID RIESMAN

Chapter Four: The Language of Layoffs

ACTION STEPS

1. What words do you use when you think or talk about layoffs? What word or words would you use to describe the event if you were laid off today? List it or them in your notebook. What would you say to your friends and family?
2. What words does your organization use? List them. What are the implications of the words you listed? How do they make you feel?
3. Are there other words you could use that are less emotionally loaded? List them.
4. If your organization has gone through a layoff or might go through one, think about what it means to you or would mean to you to be a survivor. How does that word make you feel? What other word could you use that is less emotionally loaded? How would it affect your attitude if you resisted using the word "survivor?"
5. Think through how you have reacted when a colleague or acquaintance has been laid off. Have you unconsciously tried to determine if that person deserved it?
6. Decide how you want to react in the future if a colleague or acquaintance is laid off. What kind of support could you give?

You must lose a fly to catch a trout.

GEORGE HERBERT

Appreciate failure for the education of it.

ANONYMOUS

Some of the best lessons we ever learn, we learn from our mistakes and failures. The error of the past is the wisdom and success of the future.

TRYON EDWARDS

After his laboratory burned, Thomas Edison told his son: "There is great value in disaster. All our mistakes are burned up. Thank God, we can start anew."

I can't wait for this to be over, so I can get started remembering how much fun it was.

ANONYMOUS

Chapter Five: The Anatomy of Loss

ACTION STEPS

1. Make a loss list. What would you lose if you lost your job? Rank the items on your list so that you can look for ways to replace or find substitutes for those things you decided were most significant to you. Use the ideas in chapters 6 through 10.
2. List also what you would take with you if you were laid off, such as specific skills, abilities, experiences, successes, awards, contacts, training, and education. This list can help offset the overwhelming feelings of loss.
3. Discuss the loss cycle with your significant other. Job loss usually is very threatening to loved ones. Ask those people to create a loss list. Get clear with your partner what personal and relationship issues—finances, daily routine, self-esteem, for example—might be magnified for each of you, should either of you be laid off.
4. Resolve to get professional help if your reactions become excessively negative.
5. Begin now to take better care of your health: achieve your ideal weight, get plenty of exercise, eliminate excessive drinking. These good habits will help you weather a job transition with your health intact. A consistent exercise program will provide a way to deal with increased stress and anxiety caused either by the fear of or the reality of being laid off.

Liberty means responsibility. That is why most men dread it.

GEORGE BERNARD SHAW

What is your destiny? When will you decide?

PETER BLOCK

Chapter Six: Liberate Your Mind

ACTION STEPS

1. Write down the unwritten assumptions, agreements, and bargains you notice in your relationship with your employer. To get started, look back at pages 92 through 97 and write, "If I . . . then you . . ."
2. Look back at the characteristics of the old contract on pages 94 through 97 and the new contract on pages 98 through 102. Make a list of the goodies you'll miss as you give up the old contract.
3. Plan now to be ready the next time someone asks you, "What do you do?" Talk about your skills and accomplishments, not the company you work for.
4. Set your career goals and look for ways to achieve them as you accomplish your company's goals.
5. Give 10 percent of your time to enhancing your career. Choose how to use the time most productively to create more career security for yourself.
6. Have your own business card designed and printed. It will symbolize your independent identity apart from your company affiliation.
7. Earn some amount—any amount—of money outside your job this year as a symbol of your liberation.
8. Write your own new contract to clarify the agreements you'd like to have between you and your employer. See examples on pages 110 through 112.

Money often costs too much.

RALPH WALDO EMERSON

When prosperity comes, do not use all of it.

CONFUCIUS

Want is a growing giant whom the coat of Have was never large enough to cover.

RALPH WALDO EMERSON

We work to become, not to acquire.

ELBERT HUBBARD

Chapter Seven: Line Up Your Finances

ACTION STEPS

1. Use your notebook or journal to get a handle on your money mentality and to explore and question your assumptions about your relationship with money.
2. Find people you can talk with about financial matters: family members, mentors, friends, instructors, professionals.
3. Create your own Money Manifesto, a statement that expresses your determination to take charge of your financial future, now.
4. Decide how to improve your financial IQ:

    - Hire professional help
    - Listen to audiotapes
    - Read books and magazines
    - Take a course

5. Review your company's benefits handbook. If your spouse is employed, review your spouse's benefits at the same time. Be sure you are signed up on both health plans, so that if one of you is laid off you still have insurance coverage. You may want to purchase additional disability insurance or life insurance coverage.
6. Review any documents you signed as a condition of employment. Did you, for example, sign a non compete agreement when you went to work for the company? What restrictions does it place on you? Review the agreement with an attorney. Are you prohibited from going to work for a competitor, starting your own businesses, hiring former coworkers, or taking customers with you when you leave the company?
7. Review any policies that deal with severance. If your company did let you go, what could you expect in terms of a severance package? If official policies are difficult to obtain,

talk to people who have already been laid off from your organization or a similar organization in your industry.

8. Assess your assets and liabilities. Get a financial statement form and add up your assets and liabilities or work with a professional to do this step. Figure out your annual and monthly income and expenses, dividing all expenses into fixed, flexible, and frills so that you can manage them.
9. Make your plan. Figure out how you will immediately take steps to spend less, earn more, and manage better.
10. Decide which professionals you need to develop relationships with: a lawyer, CPA, financial advisor, etc. (Note: This book is not a substitute for having professional advisors who can work with you to create a plan tailored to your needs. To find a financial advisor, get in touch with the National Association of Personal Financial Advisors, 1130 Lake Cook Road, Suite 150, Buffalo Grove, IL 60089; 800/366-2732. To find a lawyer and CPA, ask your networking contacts.)

The brighter you are the more you have to learn.

DON HEROLD

When Aristotle was asked how much educated men were superior to the uneducated, he replied, "As much as the living are to the dead."

DIONYSIUS OF HALICARNASSUS, ARISTOTLE

The only person who is educated is the one who has learned how to learn . . . and change.

CARL ROGERS

Learn as if you'll live forever; live as if you'll die tomorrow.

UNKNOWN

CHAPTER EIGHT: LEARN FOR MASTERY

ACTION STEPS

1. Consider what it would take for you to become an expert in your field. You might wish to interview someone you consider an expert to determine how that person developed his or her knowledge.
2. Determine life skills you want to acquire or polish and job skills you want to master, using the suggestions on pages 144 to 147.
3. Discover where and how to fill those skill gaps, using the list of 101 learning opportunities, starting on page 150.
4. Draft your plan. It can be as far-reaching as a five-year plan that includes a graduate degree or as short-term as a plan for this quarter. Avoid a scattershot approach that confuses activity with action. Include your goals and how you will achieve them.
5. Do the work. Make sure your plan has deadlines and checkpoints to keep you moving ahead and that activities appear regularly in your planning calendar.
6. Document your achievements by creating and keeping your learning log.
7. Once a quarter, review your plan and the steps you have taken to develop your expertise.
8. Demonstrate your expertise by volunteering, teaching, mentoring, writing, consulting, or speaking.

A human being should be able to change a diaper, plan an invasion, butcher a hog, conn a ship, design a building, write a sonnet, balance accounts, build a wall, set a bone, comfort the dying, take orders, give orders, cooperate, act alone, solve equations, analyze a new problem, pitch manure, program a computer, cook a tasty meal, fight efficiently, die gallantly. Specialization is for insects.

ROBERT A. HEINLEIN, *The Notebooks of Lazarus Long*

Anyone who can spell a word only one way is an idiot.

W. C. FIELDS

Chapter Nine: Lean Out of Specialization

ACTION STEPS

1. Attend meetings or join professional associations in the career areas you are exploring.
2. Attend the convention or conference of the career option you're exploring.
3. Look for training offered by your current employer that will expand your career options and open up adjacencies.
4. Eradicate "It's not in my job description" from your vocabulary and look for assignments, committees, or special task forces that take you outside your area of responsibility or department. Develop a broader knowledge of what your organization does and how your skills could be useful in other departments.
5. Use the library to explore adjacent or far-flung career options. Look at professional and trade magazines in other fields. Explore the wealth of materials for entrepreneurs and home-based businesspeople.
6. Join or start a career support group for people who are in career transition.

I not only use all the brains I have, but all that I can borrow.

WOODROW WILSON

It's one of the most beautiful compensations of this life that no man can sincerely try to help another without helping himself.

RALPH WALDO EMERSON

Stability comes from your network and reputation. . . . The new security resides in the network you're a part of . . . not your logo.

TOM PETERS

Chapter Ten: Link Up with People

ACTION STEPS

1. Review the quiz on page 198.
2. Learn and practice

   - Showing up
   - Meeting and greeting people
   - Creating an agenda
   - Experimenting with tapping into the six-million-person network
   - Practicing the protocol
   - Listening effectively

   NOTE: If you feel you need additional help with networking skills, see chapter 12, "Resources," for information on how to order our books on networking, *Great Connections: Small Talk and Networking for Businesspeople* and *52 Ways to Re-Connect, Follow Up, & Stay in Touch . . . When You Don't Have Time to Network.*
3. Take your calendar and plan out the time you will devote to networking activities in the next month.
4. List the organizations you currently belong to. Review the questions on page 222 to decide if you want to join other organizations.
5. Go over the questions on page 222 to decide how to become more visible in the organizations you belong to. Create your plan to increase the number of people who know you and work on it systematically.
6. Network inside your organization to become known and to get the job done faster and more efficiently.

Chapter 12

Resources

People and print are your two best sources of professional and career information. Whoever you need to know, somebody you know knows somebody who knows them. And whatever you need to know, it's available at the library or on-line via computer. And don't forget all the video and audiotape resources, which are just too numerous to mention here.

Career Management

Bridges, William, *JobShift: How to Prosper in a Workplace Without Jobs* (Redding, MA: Addison-Wesley, 1994).

Brown, Charles, James Hamilton, and James Medoff. *Employers Large and Small* (Boston, MA: Harvard University Press, 1991).

Charland, William. *Career Shifting: Starting Over in a Changing Economy* (Holbrook, MA: Bob Adams, 1993).

Burton, Mary Lindley and Richard A. Wedemeyer, *In Transition* (New York: HarperBusiness, 1991).

Cothan, James. *Career Shock: Make Your Career Happen for You . . . Not to You* (New York: Donald Fine, Inc., 1989).

Dail, Hilda Lee. *The Lotus and the Pool: How to Create*

Your Own Career (Boston, MA: Shambhala Publications, 1989).

Dubrin, Andrew J. *Bouncing Back: How to Stay in the Game When Your Career Is on the Line* (New York: McGraw-Hill, 1992).

Fox, Paul G., *Thriving in Tough Times: Smart Ways to Make Yourself More Valuable and Less Vulnerable in the Job Market of the 90s* (New York: Career Press, Inc., 1992).

Fromm, William. *The Ten Commandments of Business and How to Break Them: Secrets for Improving Employee Morale, Enhancing Customer Service, Increasing Company Profits While Having More Fun Than You Ever Thought You Could Have at Work* (New York: Berkley, 1992).

Glassner, Barry, *Career Crash: The End of America's Love Affair With Work* (New York: Simon & Schuster, 1994).

Hochheiser, Robert, *If You Want Guarantees, Buy a Toaster: Coping With Corporate Change* (New York: William Morrow, 1991).

Holloway, Diane, and Nancy Bishop. *Before You Say "I Quit": A Guide to Making Successful Job Transitions* (New York: Collier Books, 1990).

Jackson, Tom. *Guerrilla Tactics in the New Job Market* (New York: Bantam Books, 1991).

Jackson, Tom. *Not Just Another Job: How to Invent a Career That Works for You—Now and in the Future* (New York: Times Books, 1992).

Kanter, Rosabeth Moss. *When Giants Learn to Dance: Mastering the Challenge of Strategy, Management and Careers in the 1990s* (New York: Simon and Schuster, 1989).

Kolnow, Emily, and Lynne Dumans. *Congratulations! You've Been Fired: Sound Advice for Women Who've Been Terminated, Pink-Slipped, Downsized or Otherwise Unemployed* (New York: Fawcett Columbine, 1990).

Krannich, Ronald L. *Careering and Re-Careering for the 1990s: The Complete Guide to Planning Your Future* (Manassas Park, VA: Impact Publications, 1991).

Lucht, John. *Rites of Passage at $100,000 Plus: Insider's Lifetime Guide to Executive Job-Changing and Faster Career*

Progress (New York: Viceroy Press, 1993).

McMakin, Jacqueline, with Sonya Dyer. *Working from the Heart: For Those Who Hunger for Meaning and Satisfaction in Their Work* (San Diego, CA: LuraMedia, 1989).

Newman, Katherine. *Declining Fortunes: The Withering of the American Dream* (New York: HarperCollins, 1993).

Noer, David M., *Healing the Wounds: Overcoming the Trauma of Layoffs and Revitalizing Downsized Organizations* (San Francisco: Jossey-Bass, 1993).

Pedersen, Laura. *Street Smart Career Guide: A Step-by-Step Program for Your Career Development* (New York: Crown Trade Paperbacks, 1993).

Popcorn, Faith. *The Popcorn Report: On the Future of Your Company, Your World, Your Life* (New York: HarperCollins Publishers, Inc., 1992).

Rummler, Geary, and Alan Brache. *Improving Performance: How to Manage the White Space on the Organization Chart* (San Francisco: Jossey-Bass, 1990).

Sinetar, Marsha. *Do What You Love, the Money Will Follow: Discovering Your Right Livelihood* (New York: Paulist Press, 1987).

Stern, Paul, and Tom Shachtman. *Straight to the Top* (New York: Warner Books, 1990).

Wexley, Kenneth N., and Stanley B. Silverman. *Working Scared: Achieving Success in Trying Times* (San Francisco: Jossey-Bass, 1993).

Magazines and Newsletters

John Naisbitt's Trend Letter, published by The Global Network, 1101 Thirtieth Street NW, Suite 130, Washington, DC 20007; $195/yr. 800/368-0115 or 202/337-5960.

Liberate Your Mind

Aburdene, Patricia, and John Naisbitt. *Megatrends for Women* (New York: Villar Press, 1992).

Bardwick, Judith M. *The Plateauing Trap: How to Avoid It in Your Career and Your Life* (New York: American

Management Association, 1986).
Block, Peter. *The Empowered Manager: Positive Political Skills at Work* (San Francisco: Jossey-Bass Publishers, 1987).
Block, Peter. *Stewardship: Choosing Service Over Self-interest* (San Francisco: Berrett-Koehler, 1993).
Bridges, William. *Managing Transitions: Making the Most of Change* (Reading, MA: Addison-Wesley Publishing Company, 1991).
Branden, Nathaniel. *The Six Pillars of Self-esteem* (New York: Bantam Books, 1994).
Byhan, William C., and Jeff Cox. *Zapp! The Lightning of Empowerment* (New York: Fawcett, 1992).
Dubrin, Andrew. *Your Own Worst Enemy: How to Overcome Career Self-Sabotage* (New York: American Management Association, 1992).
Naisbitt, John. *Megatrends: Ten New Directions Transforming Our Lives* (New York: Warner Books, 1982).
Naisbitt, John, and Patricia Aburdene. *Reinventing the Corporation* (New York: Warner Books, 1986).
Peters, Tom. *Liberation Management* (New York: Knopf, 1992).
Saltzman, Amy. *Downshifting: Reinventing Success on a Slower Track* (New York: HarperCollins, 1991).
Simon, Sidney. *Getting Unstuck: Breaking Through the Barriers to Change* (New York: Warner, 1988).

Line Up Your Finances

Briles, Judith. *Financial Savvy for Women: A Money Book for Women of All Ages* (New York: MasterMedia, 1992).
Byers, Patricia, Julia Preston, and Patricia Johnson. *The Kid's Money Book: Great Money Making Ideas* (Cockeysville, MD: Liberty Publications, 1983).
Chopra, Deepak. *Ageless Body, Timeless Mind: The Quantum Alternative to Growing Old* (New York: Harmony, 1993).
Chopra, Deepak. *Quantum Healing: Exploring the Frontiers of Mind/Body/Medicine* (New York: Bantam, 1989).
Claflin, Edward, and Tony Hom. *Smart, Successful and*

Broke: The Six Step Action Plan for Getting Out of Debt and Into the Money (New York: Dell Publishing, 1991).

Dacyczyn, Amy. *The Tightwad Gazette: Promoting Thrift as a Viable Alternative Lifestyle* (New York: Villard Books, 1992).

Dolan, Ken, and Daria Dolan. *Straight Talk on Money: Ken and Daria Dolan's Guide to Family Money Management* (New York: Simon & Schuster, 1993).

Dominguez, Joe, and Vicki Robin. *Your Money or Your Life: Transforming Your Relationship with Money and Achieving Financial Independence* (New York: Viking, 1992).

Forward, Susan and Craig Buck, *Money Demons: How to Keep Them From Sabotaging Your Relationships and You* (New York: Bantam Books, 1994).

Mellon, Olivia. *Money Harmony: Resolving Money Conflicts in Your Life and Your Relationships* (New York: Walker & Company, 1994).

Morris, Kenneth. *The Wall Street Journal Guide to Understanding Personal Finance* (New York: Simon & Schuster, Fireside, 1993).

Phillips, Michael. *The Seven Laws of Money* (New York: Random House, 1974).

Quinn, Jane Bryant. *Making the Most of Your Money: Smart Ways to Create Wealth and Plan Your Finances in the '90s* (New York: Simon & Schuster, 1991).

Simmons, Lee, and Barbara Simmons. *Penny Pinching* (New York: Bantam Books, 1991).

Magazines

Kiplinger's Personal Finance Magazine, 1729 H Street NW, Washington, DC 20006; $18/yr.; 800/544-0155.

Money Magazine, The Time Inc. Magazine Company, Time & Life Building, Rockefeller Center, New York, NY 10020; $35.95/yr.; 800/633-9970

Smart Money, The Wall Street Journal Magazine of Personal Business, Hearst Corporation and Dow Jones & Company, Inc.; P.O. Box 7538, Red Oak, IA 51591; $24/yr.; 800/444-4204.

Newsletters

Banker's Secret Bulletin (Quarterly), Box 78, Elizaville, NY 12523; $19.95 for two years. For sample, send $1 and stamped, self-addressed envelope.

Cheapskate Monthly, P.O. Box 2135, Paramount, CA 90723; $12.95/year.

Penny Pincher, P.O. Box 809, Kings Park, NY 11754-0809; $12/year. For a free copy, send a stamped, self-addressed envelope.

Skinflint News, 1460 Noell Blvd., Palm Harbor, FL 34683-5639; $9.95/year. For a free copy, send a stamped, self-addressed envelope.

Straight Talk on Your Money, Phillips Publishing International, 7811 Montrose Rd., Potomac, MD 20854; $39.50/yr. To subscribe, call 800/777-2002.

Tightwad Gazette, R.R. 1, Box 3570, Leeds, ME 04263; $12/year. For a free copy, send a stamped, self-addressed envelope.

Learn for Mastery

Adams, Kathleen. *Journey to the Self: 22 Paths to Personal Growth* (New York: Warner, 1990).

Armstrong, Thomas. *Seven Kinds of Smart: Identifying and Developing Your Many Intelligences* (New York: Penguin Books, 1993).

Covey, Stephen R. *The Seven Habits of Highly Effective People* (New York: Simon & Schuster, 1990).

Dryden, Gordon and Jeannette Vos, editors, *Learning Revolution: A Life-Long Learning Program for the World's Finest Computer: Your Amazing Brain* (Torrance, CA: Jalmar Press, 1994).

Leonard, George. *Mastery: The Keys to Long-Term Success and Fulfillment* (New York: New American Library, Dutton, 1992).

Senge, Peter M. *The Fifth Discipline: The Art and Practice of the Learning Organization* (New York: Doubleday, 1990).

Wick, Calhoun, and Lu Stanton Leon. *The Learning Edge: How Smart Managers and Smart Companies Stay Ahead* (New York: McGraw-Hill, 1993).

Lean Out of Specialization

Bermer, Jeff. *The Joy of Working from Home: Making a Life While Making a Living* (San Francisco: Berrett-Koehler, 1994).

Carroll, Andrew. *Volunteer USA: A Comprehensive Guide to Worthy Causes That Need You* (New York: Fawcett Columbine, 1991).

Edwards, Paul, and Sarah Edwards. *The Best Home Businesses for the '90s: The Inside Information You Need to Know to Select a Home-Based Business That's Right for You* (New York: J. P. Tarcher, 1991). To order, call 800/325-6149.

Edwards, Paul, and Sarah Edwards. *Making It on Your Own: Surviving and Thriving on the Ups and Downs of Being Your Own Boss* (New York: J. P. Tarcher, 1991). To order, call 800/325-6149.

Edwards, Paul, and Sarah Edwards. *Working from Home: Everything You Need to Know About Living and Working Under the Same Roof* (New York: J. P. Tarcher, 1990). To order, call 800 325-6149.

Fanning, John and Rosemary Maniscalco, *Workstyles to Fit Your Lifestyle* (Englewood Cliffs, NJ: Prentice Hall, 1993).

Godfrey, Joline. *Our Wildest Dreams: Women Entrepreneurs Making Money, Having Fun, Doing Good: A Whole New Definition of Success and an Entirely New Paradigm of Working Life* (New York: Harper Business Books, 1993).

Henderson, David G. *Job Search: Marketing Your Military Experience in the 1990s* (Harrisburg, PA: Stackpole Books, 1991).

Justice, Peggy O'Connell, *The Temp Track: Make One of the Hottest Job Trends of the 90s Work for You* (Princeton, NJ: R. R. Bowker, 1994).

Manning, Barbralu. *Kids Mean Business: How to Turn Your Love of Children into a Profitable and Wonderfully Satisfying*